Lloyds TSB
International

Wherever you work

AXA PPP healthcare is right there with you

Resident expatriate or local national... working, travelling or retired: when you're living abroad you deserve top quality healthcare from a well grounded company that really knows their way around the world of private health!

AXA PPP healthcare has an International Health Plan to suit your needs. Join us and you can rely on quick, easy access to private medical treatment; a choice of hospitals; emergency evacuation or repatriation; plus an English-speaking health information line that's on call for you around-the-clock.

For great British healthcare – worldwide – join us now and we'll give you two months' cover free

Call +44(0)1892 550817 quoting reference WA2006 or visit www.axappphealthcare.co.uk/wa

All claims will be assessed against the terms and conditions of the chosen product and any individual exclusions placed on your policy at joining.

PPP HEALTHCARE

——— Be Life Confident ———

Contents

"I feel **special** because they speak to me in **my language**"

If you need to make a claim, would you want to speak to someone who will understand your needs? To get the feeling, there's only one number to call.

THE QUEEN'S AWARDS FOR ENTERPRISE: INTERNATIONAL TRADE 2005

BUPA International

24 hour multi-lingual helpline

Call +44 (0) 1273 208181
www.bupa-intl.com

Your calls will be recorded and may be monitored.

Demand for understanding English is vast. Get back to school!

One of the most rewarding ways to experience a foreign country is to work as an English teacher. Suddenly you're no longer a tourist – you're a valuable part of your students' lives, giving them access to the world's media and information.

The British Council has a network of teaching centres in over 100 cities worldwide. We teach English to children and adults at all levels, and special courses for companies – such as airlines, hotels, petrochemical technicians and journalists, and public services including lawyers and the military. For all these students we need imaginative and inspiring teachers.

Teachers working for the British Council need a degree in any subject and a qualification in English language teaching, such as the Cambridge CELTA or Trinity College TESOL certificate. These qualifications are taught in several different countries and in the UK. Have a look at the websites at the end of this feature to see where.

Working for a British Council school, teachers benefit from very good terms and conditions and lots of encouragement to develop professionally. Our contracts are usually for two years in any one city and unlike other schools we encourage teachers to move around our own network.

We are a non-political organisation concerned with building lasting relationships. The lessons we teach and learn endure through political and economic upheavals, and our teachers are thoroughly engaged in our public diplomacy role. To find out more about us, or how to become a Teacher of EFL, please visit our website **http://trs.britishcouncil.org**

Useful websites:
Cambridge ESOL **www.cambridgeesol.org**
Trinity College London **www.trinitycollege.co.uk**
Professional TEFL jobseekers site **www.tefl.com**
Helpful resource for all things TEFL **www.cactustefl.com**

BRITISH COUNCIL

Be different. English language teachers who work overseas for the British Council play an essential part in reflecting the diversity of modern Britain. We recognise that people from all backgrounds, ages and faiths bring valuable skills and experience to our teaching centres. If you would like to know more about teaching English as a Foreign Language for an organisation that values different people please e-mail us on teacher.vacancies@britishcouncil.org, telephone 020 7389 4931 or visit our website **http://trs.britishcouncil.org**

The British Council's Child Protection policy requires that any appointment is contingent on thorough checks. In the UK, and in other countries where appropriate systems exist, these include criminal records checks.

BRITISH COUNCIL

TEACH THERE

DOLPHIN MOVERS

Dolphin Movers is a long-established UK based fully integrated overseas moving company providing global moving solutions for private individuals and for organisations with an internationally mobile workforce.

For over 15 years, we have been responsible for moving thousands of peoples possessions to and from the UK to every destination you could possibly imagine.

Why are we so popular?

- We can move your belongings to anywhere, from anywhere, by land, sea or air.
- We offer a stress-free export packing service at residence.
- We handle export formalities and documentation, insurance coverage and overseas Customs, and will manage your move from packing to unpacking.
- We offer short and long term storage in the UK and at destination.
- Our management team have over 100 years experience between them.
- We have a network of 390 trusted agents across the world carefully selected.
- We always aim to offer the most competitive pricing in the market.
- We always provide a professional, personal and reliable stress free service.

You are moving house and naturally want the best for your move. So do we. That's why we are proud members of the British Association of Removers (BAR). Entry to the BAR is strictly subject to us reaching high standards in our financial and operational dealings within the industry. As adherents to their Code of Practice, which is designed to protect our customers, you can rest assured that we reach the highest possible standards at all times.

AROUND THE GLOBE OR AROUND THE CORNER? YOU'LL GET THE SAME GREAT SERVICE FROM DOLPHIN MOVERS
Here at Dolphin Movers, we help people relocate for work or pleasure,

within Europe and around the globe. You see, we can move anything, anywhere; by sea, land or air. What's more, we can even help you with customs formalities, all documentation requirements, as well as other export or import formalities. We always save our customers time, and take the stress out of moving.

PACKING UP: WE'LL CARE FOR YOUR BELONGINGS AS IF THEY WERE OUR OWN

As specialists in international moving, all our export packing crews are fully trained, experienced and up to date in all the latest packing techniques. In January 2005 and 2006 we were presented with The National Guild award for excellence in respect of removals, storage and export packing.

Our packaging materials are all purpose made to protect your belongings whilst in transit. We use showerproofed padded blanket furniture wrap, acid-free tissue paper, sturdy corrugated sheets and bubble wrap, as well as a vast array of reinforced cartons, jiffy foam and extra strong sealing tape.

We also have export cartons specifically made for certain items, such as wardrobe cartons for hanging your clothing and keeping them crease free, smaller cartons for heavier objects and larger cartons for lighter objects.

As you'd expect, we pack fragile items including fine art, antiques, pianos, grandfather clocks, glass display cabinets, paintings and so on using the appropriate materials. Packages are then cased or crated for added protection. We can also design and build made-to-measure timber crates and cases tailored to your needs.

Of course, we would be happy to provide suitable packing materials to help you if you would like to pack some items yourself.

TRACKING YOUR SHIPMENT: OUR ATTENTION TO DETAIL IS METICULOUS

Once we've finished packing, our packing crew will clearly label every item with our computerised labels. These feature an item number, your name, reference number and final destination details. Our crew will also supply you with a numbered inventory list containing the contents of each box packed. If relevant, this list will also be sent to our agents at your destination to ensure that all pieces are safely delivered.

Once we've labelled all your items, every piece will then be loaded either in to our specialised removal vehicle or into a sea-freight container.

"I was very impressed with the efficient, professional and speedy way you have dealt with my move and wouldn't hesitate to recommend you. Thank you once again." *Georgina Fitzgerald (London, UK to Kalkan, Turkey)*

AT YOUR NEW HOME: EVERYTHING WILL ARRIVE SAFE AND SOUND

We have a global network of experienced agents in over 100 countries, personally selected to perform the very important final stage of your move. In most instances we have personally visited their facilities to ensure they meet our exacting standards.

When your belongings arrive at your final destination, our agents will make contact with you to arrange a convenient delivery date and time. At the stated time, they will unload and unpack all your furniture into all relevant rooms and remove all used packing materials and debris.

"We received our container ten days ago – on time and in perfect condition. It was not our first move in and out of Israel but this was the best service we've ever received from any company." *Oded Drory (London to Israel)*

STORAGE: SAFE, CLEAN ND SECURE

We offer short and long-term containerised storage facilities within our H.M. Revenue & Customs approved storage depository. All our storage facilities are fully secured, benefiting from CCTV and red care alarm systems.

If you are moving from the UK, your packed items and furniture will be delivered to our depot. Then, depending on your requirements, we can store your items in the UK, can ship them to your new residence, or can store them in a secure facility at final destination.

We offer all customers four weeks storage free of charge for all booked shipments not leaving the UK immediately. We can also offer you storage insurance for your stored items.

INSURANCE: JUST IN CASE...

Although we will take every care with your belongings, we recommend that all our customers take out relevant insurance. We are Authorised and

Regulated by The Financial Services Authority (FSA), and are able to arrange marine transit insurance cover underwritten by Lloyds of London specifically designed to insure household goods, personal effects and motor vehicles whilst in transit.

BAGGAGE SHIPPING: FOR THOSE ITEMS THAT YOU JUST CAN'T DO WITHOUT
Whether you are moving a complete household or have a small shipment consisting of a few cartons we are able to offer highly competitive rates either by sea, air or road transport depending on the destination and urgency. We provide free packaging materials to include cartons, bubble wrap and tape.

WANT A SMOOTH MOVE? TRUST DOLPHIN MOVERS
Why not give us a ring today for a free no obligation home survey? We will then arrange for one of our friendly surveyors to make an appointment to come to your home and talk to you about your move, and the items you are going to be taking.

Within 48 hours of our visit you will receive our written estimate for a full door-to-door service. We will then allocate you a Move Manager who will make all necessary arrangements and help with any questions or queries you might have.

For a smooth move, please contact us today and get your move off to the best possible start. Why not give us a call now on freephone **0800 032 9777**.

Dolphin Movers Ltd	Phone: 020 8804 7700
2 Haslemere Business Centre	Fax: 020 8804 3232
Lincoln Way	Email: sales@dolphinmovers.com
Enfield	Web: www.dolphinmovers.com
Middlesex EN1 1TE	

Individual country profiles can be found on the Kogan Page website.
Weblink: www.koganpage.com/workingabroad
Password: WA50571

MOVING ABROAD?
Don't be lost for words...

Language learning hints and tips from the experts

1. Work at your own pace
Don't try to do too much at once – half an hour a few times a week is a great start.

2. Enlist a partner
Try to persuade a friend or family member to study with you, and agree times to meet and test each other regularly.

3. A little language goes a long way
Even if you feel unsure about your ability to form correct, complete sentences, you'll find that you can make yourself understood with just a few words – and with practice you'll soon become more fluent.

4. Speak, speak, speak
Practise speaking as often as you can. Try recording yourself and reading aloud: this will help you memorize vocabulary and structures.

5. Build up your vocabulary
Aim to learn six or seven words at a time to widen your vocabulary gradually – don't overload with too many at once.

6. Immerse yourself in the language
Watch films with subtitles, listen to a foreign radio station, or watch foreign language TV programmes – they are a great way of getting used to sounds and intonations.

7. Get the right tools
You will need a good dictionary to help translate new words and expressions as you expand your vocabulary. Oxford's range of bilingual dictionaries gives you plenty of translation clues through the use of examples, plus extra help with grammar and usage.

For more language learning resources, visit
www.askoxford.com/languages

OXFORD
UNIVERSITY PRESS

Acknowledgements

Over the years many individuals and organisations have helped us with information and advice on various aspects of working and living abroad, and in updating information for successive editions. We wish to extend our thanks to the British Council; to the European Council of International Schools; Towers Perrin; BDO Stoy Hayward LLP; Lloyds TSB Bank; the Association of Residential Letting Agents; Chelstoke International; the members of foreign embassies and high commissions in London and the press offices of various government departments (particularly DSS, DfES, HMRC) who have helped in the revision of the text; and readers who have written in with criticisms, information and suggestions.

Introduction

THE JOB OUTLOOK FOR UK EXPATRIATES

British expatriates are still highly regarded abroad and their salary rates are competitive against labour recruited from the United States and most Western European countries which joined the European Union (EU) but not the 12 since 30 April 2004. However, the overseas job markets for British knowledge workers and managers have become increasingly tough, and US and European contractors still turn to the United Kingdom to recruit skilled workers for both their short- and longer-term projects overseas at rates of remuneration not necessarily below those demanded by their own nationals. This type of contract is normally lucrative for the UK national and has the added advantage that the contractor frequently provides good living conditions and contractual benefits.

The ability to earn significant salaries overseas, together with the chance to avoid UK taxes, sounds like Utopia. However, the expatriate worker is faced with a new set of problems. Many of these will be outside the work assignment itself and will involve his or her family and social life. Working abroad requires a substantial adjustment in attitudes towards work and life in general. The ability to adapt to the new environment is absolutely essential, together with a willingness to make the best of things as they are in the new surroundings. Attempting to change that environment to your own country's way of life is doomed to failure and will cause the resentment of the host country.

Lucrative overseas employment can solve many problems and may seem like the answer to a prayer. But it also creates human problems that may result in broken marriages, ruined careers and disturbed children. In accepting a job overseas you are taking a considerable risk and you should calculate how big the risk is in your particular case. Very often you will find that there is a direct correlation between risk and reward. For example, working for a major company such as British Aerospace in Saudi Arabia, with the benefit of a more secure environment at work and company housing, ought to carry much less risk than working for a Saudi company. The rate of pay offered may be very different, with the Saudi company offering much higher pay, but without the security and facilities which British Aerospace would provide. However, even working for British Aerospace will not stop or cure all the problems caused by working overseas. It will also not give workers immunity if they break the laws of the host country; nor, as we are all too well aware, does it provide immunity from acts of international terrorism.

People work overseas for many different reasons and are motivated by so many different things. It is difficult to believe anyone who says that money is not one of the major incentives. The duration of overseas employment is also varied. Some people just work a one- or two-year contract to help pay off the mortgage, or to produce the capital to start a business. Others engage in a series of shorter-term project assignments, often hopping from one country to another. However, such short-term contracts attract many applications and usually tend to be taken up by 'permanent expatriates' – those people who have spent much of their working lives abroad and migrate from one assignment to another.

The risks of working overseas for extended periods were enhanced by a Court of Appeal decision (24 January 2004), which said that rights contained in the 1996 Employment Rights Act were designed to cover 'employment in Great Britain'.

The unfair dismissal rights of expat workers has been a grey area of employment law, particularly since a section of the 1996 Act was repealed without replacement more than three years ago. Hitherto, judges had ruled that employees working abroad should be able to pursue unfair dismissal claims in the UK if their employment had a 'substantial connection' with Great Britain, a much looser interpretation, which the Court of Appeal said that it did not accept.

Increasingly, though, employers are looking to replace expatriation with short-term assignments, often to train suitably qualified local nationals on the job, or even commuting to locations, where practically possible. New technology has encouraged such changes and the introduction of 'virtual assignments' has meant that professionals can manage projects from their own country, with regular visits to their international office. While this might avoid the problems traditional models of expatriation face – such as the upheaval of family and home – an entirely new set of problems arise, such as the burden of frequent travel.

Career development is another common reason for working abroad and is particularly important for those working in multinational and international companies, government bodies, banks and organisations with large export markets.

An expatriate returning to the UK faces as many adjustments to life and work as he or she does in going out to an overseas job. Picking up the threads of a career in the UK can be extremely difficult and overseas experience is not always regarded favourably. Employers with no previous experience in overseas work themselves may think that you are returning from a very alien environment with outdated technology and human relations practices no longer acceptable in the EU, and doubt your ability to cope with new technology and life in the UK. In reality, there is little or no job security for returning expatriates, as Stephen Gill explains in Chapter 3.

Recruiting organisations need to find workers who can perform a specified job in an overseas environment. It is easy to find candidates who can do the job in a British environment but only a small proportion can survive and succeed overseas. Their second task is to ensure that any applicant they select is aware of all the problems and difficulties he or she is likely to encounter in the country where he or she is going to work. They do not want the candidate to be surprised by conditions when he or she arrives, resulting in a premature termination of contract. This is bad for the individual and may affect his or her future employment prospects. It is bad for the company since it is very disruptive and involves them in substantial replacement costs. It is also bad for the recruitment agent since it undermines the confidence of the client company, which can turn totally against the idea of using British workers.

Given that you have decided, after careful consideration of your family and your career, to find work overseas, you will need to identify the best way of achieving this, and to decide in which overseas countries you wish to work. Working in the Middle East is very different from working in Africa, which is also poles apart from working in the United States, Europe or Asia. Carrying out research on your host country before departure will help, and the resource section (contained on the Kogan Page website) will help get you started on this. However, more often than not it is not until you arrive in your new home that the differences in work and home environment, and whether or not you will be able to fit in comfortably, will become apparent.

CHANGES IN OVERSEAS JOB MARKETS

The overall number of jobs for UK expatriates has declined significantly in the past 20 years. Before that the jobs most affected were for unskilled, semi-skilled, clerical and administrative workers, many of which are now filled by workers from South East Asia and the Indian sub-continent where wage rates are much lower, or outsourced where possible to the same locations. However, even high-wage professional jobs have now migrated to low-cost countries where educational and skills standards are high as a result of the trend towards global outsourcing in service industries.

This trend has been strongest in IT services, particularly in call centre activities related to commercial and investment banking and other service industries where there is a high usage of information technology systems management and data transactions. India, with its pool of well-educated, English-speaking workers, is at the forefront of these developments, together with Australia, Malaysia, Singapore and, increasingly, China. South Africa, too, is offering opportunities for offshore relocation. As the migration of white-collar work moves up the value chain from call centre operators to occupations such as equity research, accounting, computer programming and chip design, there is a clear threat to domestic jobs employing those skills. There may be limited opportunities for British expats in the short term in setting up and managing these service facilities but salaries are unlikely to be more than 10–20 per cent above current UK rates. Of course, the ability to avoid tax and deductions from salary and the receipt of free accommodation and other benefits may still make such contracts financially attractive.

Other movements in overseas job markets have taken place nearer to home. On 1 May 2004 the EU was enlarged from 15 to 25 members with the long-awaited accession of Cyprus, the Czech Republic, Estonia, Hungary, Latvia, Lithuania, Malta, Poland, Slovakia and Slovenia. More recently, on 1 January 2007 the accession of Bulgaria and Romania increased EU membership to 27. At one level opportunities for British managers in professional firms and foreign-invested enterprises are declining as local management skills and experience grow. However, for those seeking employment or considering a change of residence to any of those countries, the level playing field of EU membership should apply in terms of employment law and social services, making relocation possible if income differentials are accepted.

So far, the traffic from the new EU member states, notably Poland, has been largely one-way. Well-educated and skilled nationals from those countries take up work in the UK to gain experience and to enjoy the benefit of higher wages and salaries before returning home to work there. This temporary migration does nothing to increase job opportunities abroad for British citizens.

FAMILY CONSIDERATIONS

Perhaps the most fundamental question an expatriate must resolve is whether he or she is going to take up a post on an unaccompanied status or whether he or she is looking for accompanied postings. Many people who apply for overseas jobs have not thought out the problems and have not reached a family agreement on the type of posting required. One of the major irritations affecting international recruiters is that some candidates apply for single-status jobs and then at the final interview state they are only prepared to accept an accompanied status situation. This results in a complete waste of time and money for both parties and is guaranteed to reduce your chances of getting employment through that agent.

Before you even decide to apply for an overseas job you must discuss and agree with your family the status of posting that you are prepared to take, the countries you would want to work in, and the minimum remuneration and benefits package you will accept. Only when you have decided these points are you in a position to start making job applications. Furthermore, many dual-income couples will need to investigate job opportunities for an accompanying partner in the new location, as many are no longer prepared to give up their own career for the sake of a foreign sojourn. The issues affecting the 'trailing spouse' are fully discussed in Chapters 3 and 7.

USING TECHNOLOGY

Advances in communications technology have certainly made the expatriate's life easier. Keeping in contact with colleagues, friends and family can be done with ease. If you haven't already done so, become acquainted with the internet. This has become an invaluable aid for the international community and provides quick and cheap global communication. It also provides excellent information on any subject you care to think of, including country-specific information, job opportunities, government advice and so on. This book recognises the impact of the internet on the expatriate community and, where possible, website addresses for relevant information are included. For this edition, where there are no websites available we have included the postal address and telephone number instead. However, website addresses change frequently, as does the content, and we are unable to take responsibility for the accuracy of these contact details. Once you are on the right track, using the links provided by many websites, it should prove a worthwhile and fruitful journey, arming you with the information required to settle into your foreign assignment. Where websites are not given, the ubiquitous Google search engine will probably provide information.

EMPLOYEE EXPECTATIONS

Chapter 2 focuses on the opportunities that employees may be offered to work overseas for various periods and the remuneration packages to look for.

If you are not in the position of working for a company that may offer you overseas employment and do not expect to do so, you may prefer to omit this chapter from your reading. However, if you are considering company employment in an overseas operation the chapter may provide some understanding of the corporate perspective and the kinds of conditions and benefits that you may be offered.

You will note that multinationals today are looking hard at the high costs of their globally mobile staff and may be taking less generous attitudes towards benefits.

Chapter 3, an addition to past editions of *Working Abroad*, offers specific advice to those who are considering engagement in short-term overseas assignments

CONCLUSION

The rewards of moving abroad to work can be high and usually offer the chance to make significant savings. The amount of your savings depends largely on the location chosen and your attitude to life abroad.

Perhaps the expatriate who finds life the most difficult is the married person with teenage children, since in many countries secondary education is either unavailable or extremely expensive. The alternative of a UK boarding school is also expensive, and tends to break up the family unit.

We strongly recommend that if you are seriously contemplating a job overseas you should research the job market very carefully. You should try to decide whether you have the ability to survive and succeed overseas and whether, where appropriate, your family can also adapt to the new lifestyle. Once you have made this decision honestly, you must first identify the countries that offer the rewards and conditions you require and then identify the companies that might offer you employment.

NEW CONTRIBUTORS

The professional contributors to this twenty-ninth edition of *Working Abroad* have revised their texts where necessary. Philip Pertoldi of Abels Moving Services has contributed advice on practical issues of moving home, and the section on the provision of entertainment and home comforts for those far from home is provided by Expats Essentials. Advice on managing foreign exchange issues is offered by Currencies Direct, and health insurance terms available to expatriates from AXA PPP healthcare and BUPA are included.

Jonathan Wix of the Teacher Recruitment section of the British Council has updated the information on Teaching English as a Foreign Language in Chapter 1 and the 'From expat to expert' section of Chapter 7.

Lloyds TSB Bank has again contributed to the sections on financial planning for expatriates and the provision of international personal banking services.

For this twenty-ninth edition, my thanks also go to Stephen Gill of Stephen Gill Associates, who has contributed the new Chapter 3 on expatriate employees' expectations.

For this edition, Chapter 4 and the checklists in Part Two detailing the effects on personal taxation of working abroad, written by BDO Stoy Hayward for the twenty-seventh edition, are unchanged, as are some of the briefings on personal taxation and immigration procedures provided by their associated offices.

On the website to which your password gives you access, the number of countries surveyed stands at 60 and current detailed information on the economies of each country is provided.

Jonathan Reuvid

Part One:

Job Opportunities and Employee Expectations

1 Independent Job Opportunities

It is difficult, if not impossible, to form any precise idea of the number of UK citizens currently working overseas. Despite the flood of human resource statistics which flows from Whitehall, there is no central register of expatriates. The broad trend can, however, be adduced by examining people's intentions, looking at the range of jobs on offer, and the numbers of applications for particular posts. The peak was probably reached about 30 years ago, before rising unemployment in many countries, political risks and terrorism in the Middle East and Africa and perhaps more optimism about prospects at home combined to make people more cautious. Moreover, reductions in UK income tax rates until recently tended to reduce financial incentives to work and live overseas. In the past year, there have been signs that this trend has been reversed, with evidence of young and more mature families who find UK living conditions, taxation burdens and job prospects unattractive and decide to move abroad permanently.

However, expatriate employment, though continuing to be an attractive prospect to UK jobseekers, is no longer the Klondike it used to be. At present only the most intrepid and seasoned expatriates would consider taking up postings in most Middle East and some African countries. Economic and political problems have affected the expatriate job markets in Africa and Latin America, and opportunities for non-Chinese speakers in China or Hong Kong are increasingly limited. Multinational company appointments in China are now filled mainly by those with Chinese as a second (or first) language or by young, internationally educated Chinese people who have returned home. Compensating factors are a continuing demand in specific areas of employment, notably in the financial and retail service sectors, and the growth in short-term contracts.

This shading off has been accompanied by a trend towards greater stability in salaries, as well as some degree of uniformity in the remuneration packages being offered by different employers for comparable jobs, as competition for expatriate labour diminishes. In many parts of the world remuneration in sterling terms has only risen by the level of UK inflation.

Opportunities have diminished more markedly at technician and supervisory levels, because of competition from qualified personnel in developing countries who are prepared to accept much lower salaries, and also because of the gradual emergence of skilled workers among local nationals as the fruits of training schemes come on-stream. On the other hand, at more senior grades the relatively low level of British executive salaries by international standards continues to make UK managers an attractive proposition – especially those who are prepared to be reasonably flexible about working and living conditions. The typical US expatriate employee will often expect to take with him or her the standard of living associated with an executive lifestyle in the United States. Consequently, many senior jobs go to British or European personnel.

FINDING A JOB ABROAD

So how do you set about trying to find a job abroad? Both new and old forms of media provide ample opportunities for jobseekers looking from their home country. And for the brave, there is always the choice of turning up on spec to search out job opportunities in the chosen destination, although this approach is no longer recommended.

Newspapers

Not only the nationals and the Sunday newspapers but also the trade press carry overseas job advertisements. Graduates can look in annual career directories for details of overseas employers. It stands to reason that any employer wishing to recruit UK personnel will advertise in the UK press, but there is another good reason why the 'overseas vacancies' pages are worth scanning: they give a very good indication of the going rates of salary and benefits in particular parts of the world. Indeed, even if you have been made an offer without having replied to an advertisement, it is worth looking closely at

these pages over a few issues to make sure that the remuneration package being put to you is in line with market rates.

However, if you are actually looking for a job, do not just confine your reading to the ads. It is worth reading any news and features that relate to the countries you are interested in. Not only will news of general or specific economic developments – a new industry opening up, for instance – give you background information that might be very useful in an interview, but it might also in itself be a source of job leads. Indeed, if you can read the papers in the language of the country you would like to work in, so much the better. They will go into potential job-lead information in more depth and, of course, they contain job advertisements. How useful these are likely to be to the British jobseeker depends somewhat on the country in which the paper is published. In the Far East, for instance, employers would almost exclusively be looking for locals when advertising in a local paper. But in the EU, a response from a suitably qualified EU national might well produce a positive result. Quite a number of European countries are involved in projects in the Middle East and in other resource-rich countries where English is the dominant language. In those cases, some think in terms of putting UK nationals on location as well as their own people.

Apart from the major newspapers, some countries have also developed their equivalent of career publications. Published every two weeks, *Overseas Jobs Express*, 20 New Road, Brighton, Sussex BN1 1UF (tel: 01273 699777, fax: 01273 69977) carries international recruitment advertising and provides information and news about working abroad. This excellent paper costs £75 a year, or £29.95 for three months. *Overseas Jobs Express* also publishes several books, including *Finding a Job in Canada* and *Finding a Job in Australia*, both £9.95, as well as a number of titles for young people wanting to live and work abroad.

There are also a number of news-sheets which are advertised from time to time, but some of them, it must be said, are fly-by-night operations and you would be ill-advised to part with your money without seeing a sample copy or to subscribe for more than six months at a time.

The internet

One of the most effective ways of looking for a job abroad is to search the wide range of websites offering information for jobseekers. There are a number of ways in which the internet can help and *Online Job Hunting – Great Answers to Tough Questions* by Martin Yate and Terra Dourlain (published by Kogan Page) is a good source of help. Useful categories include:

- Careers libraries in schools, colleges and universities.
- Professional associations and journals.
- People doing the job you are interested in. You can 'talk' to people via the internet using a service such as Internet Relay Chat.
- Job advertisements, job descriptions and person specifications.
- Employers and employment agencies in the industries to which your skills and experience are relevant.
- Promotional organisations.

Many large employers have job advertisements and descriptions for every area of work and provide application forms online. Interesting sites are listed in the directory at the back of this book, but two good examples of employer websites can be found at Shell International on www.shell.com and Hewlett-Packard on www.jobs.hp.com. Another invaluable resource is The Monster Board, which has information and sites in Canada, Australia, Belgium and The Netherlands on www.monster.com. Most large employers have sites and they are well worth a visit to assess what kinds of international opportunities are available. The advantages of carrying out a job search on the internet are as follows:

- The main sources of information on vacancies are unchanged. However, they are made more accessible to all by means of the web.
- Searching for vacancies on the web should be quicker and more effective than by other means. Dedicated search tools make finding appropriate jobs in newspapers and with agencies quick and straightforward.
- There are simple ways of arranging to be notified of suitable vacancies by e-mail.
- Some employers encourage and facilitate speculative applications via their websites.
- CV databases enable you to make your skills and abilities known to a large audience of potential employers.

■ Web-based vacancy searches should enhance, not replace, other means of job hunting.

Source: *Net That Job!* **Irene Krechowiecka**

FINDING A JOB ON SPEC

Possible sources of job information are, of course, legion and they change constantly. Apart from keeping a close watch on the papers, as good a move as any is to get in touch with trade associations connected to the country in which you are interested or local chambers of commerce there. They will not be able to give you any job leads as such, unless you are very lucky, but they can usually give you lists of firms or other organisations that have a particularly close connection with the UK. Preliminary leads of this nature are essential if you are going to a country to look for a job on spec, and, except in the EU, you should never state this as your intention when entering a country. In most places now you need to have a job offer from a local employer in order to get a work permit, so you should always state that you are entering as a visitor, whatever your subsequent intention might be. It must be said, however, that some countries do not permit turning a visitor's visa into a work permit – that is something you will have to check on, discreetly, before you go.

In general, however, going abroad on spec to find a job is not a good idea. Even in the EU, where it is permitted, some jobseekers have had unhappy experiences unless they are in a 'hot' area such as electronics. By far the best plan is to get interviews lined up before you go or at least get some expressions of interest from potential employers – they will probably not commit themselves to more than that from a distance, even if there is a job possibility. To do more might put them under an embarrassing moral obligation when you turn up on their doorstep, having spent a lot of time and money to get there.

British jobseekers now have greater access to vacancies in Europe with the introduction of the EURES (European Employment Services) computer network, which provides jobseekers with free information and guidance on current opportunities throughout the EU. The database includes up-to-date information on living and working conditions in other member states. In Britain, anyone interested in working abroad can access the EURES database, and obtain advice from a Euroadviser, via their local Jobcentre. The International Job Search Advice unit of the Employment Service produces a useful information booklet *Working Abroad*, as well as a series of guides entitled *Working in…*, concerning specific countries. These deal with entry requirements, information sources, benefits, liabilities, taxation, state of the market and cultural notes. The unit also holds information on work overseas in specific professions. Write with your details to International Job Search Advice, 6th Floor, Whitehall II, Whitehall Quay, Leeds LS1 4HR (tel: 0113 309 8090) or visit www.jobcentreplus.gov.uk. Alternatively, consult the linked website www.eures-jobs.com on which job vacancies across the EU are advertised and you can post your CV and details.

Further useful information on the EU and its members can be accessed via Public Information Relays (PIR), European Documentation Centres (EDC) and Euro Info Centres (EIC) set up in libraries or at regional government offices or Business Links. Contact your local library for details of your nearest source of EU information.

Writing on-spec letters to potential employers is a subject that is well covered elsewhere. In essence what you have to do is address yourself to something that you have identified as being the employer's need or possible need – this is where researching the background on the internet and elsewhere and looking for job leads comes into play. For instance, if you have read in *Der Spiegel* or in *Frankfurter Allgemeine Zeitung* of a German firm being awarded a large contract in the Middle East, it is likely that they will respond in some way, provided your letter demonstrates that you have relevant skills and experience. Even if they intend advertising the job, the fact that you have taken an intelligent interest in their activities will count in your favour. It is seldom worthwhile advertising in the situations wanted column, though writing to headhunters is a good move, especially if you are qualified to work in one of the fields in current demand. Letters should be kept short and your CV should not exceed two pages – highlighting and quantifying achievements, rather than just listing posts you have held. With technical jobs you may have to show that your knowledge of the field is up to date with current developments, especially in areas where things are changing rapidly.

When a job is actually advertised, the interview will probably be in London, or your fare will be paid if you are called upon to travel abroad. Here again, the rules for replying to an advertisement are no different from those relating to UK employers: read the text carefully and frame your reply and organise your CV in such a way as to show that you meet the essential requirements of the job. As one Canadian employer put it recently, paraphrasing, no doubt, John F Kennedy's much quoted presidential address, 'The question to ask is not what I can gain from moving to your company, but what your company (or organisation or school) can gain from me.'

If you need to arrange your own travel, companies such as CIBT®, the global visa and passport service at www.uk.cibt.com, specialise in processing applications for business, working-holiday and tourism visas and passports on your behalf, which is particularly useful for those living outside London, where most embassies and consulates are located. Most professions have specialist agencies to help find work both nationally and internationally, and these could be a first port of call. Non-professional jobs such as au-pairing or voluntary work are also well served and details are given further on in this chapter.

SPECIALIST AREAS

Engineers and technicians

These terms cover many grades of expatriate worker, from truck drivers and road builders to site supervisors and project directors. Many overseas companies, especially airlines and construction companies, recruit directly in the UK by advertising in UK newspapers. Examine all such offers carefully. Many companies will arrange for technicians going abroad to meet compatriots on leave, who can answer their questions.

However, this is one area where opportunities are now very limited indeed. Workers from countries such as Korea, the Philippines, India and Pakistan, China and, of course, the new member states of the EU now predominate at this end of the labour market.

At the top end of the scale, the Malla Technical Recruitment Consultancy, a part of the Synergy Group, at 77 Cornhill, London EC3V 3QQ (tel: 0800 0725 900, e-mail: recruit@malla.com, website: www.malla.com) has a register of international engineering experts on all subjects who are leased out on contract worldwide.

The professionally qualified

The professions and qualifications most in demand overseas are medicine, agriculture and food, process engineering, finance, civil engineering and construction. In general, positions in these areas can best be found through the companies themselves or through management consultants and headhunters (executive search consultants). Many consultants specialise in particular professions such as accountancy.

Some are on a small, specialist scale. An example of an international, multi-purpose agency is Eurotech Associates Limited (The Old Coach House, 56 High Street, Harston, Cambridge CB2 5PZ; tel: 01223 875100, fax: 01223 875150, website: www.eurotech.org). Eurotech recruit only for the Middle East, the Far East and North Africa. They are a major international training and recruitment agency specialising in executive, managerial, technical and scientific fields. They are particularly involved with the oil industry, and their activities range from construction, maintenance and operations, engineering, oil and petrochemicals to health care, hospitals, and general financial and commercial management.

People with professional qualifications will obviously consult their appropriate professional association or trade union. In the medical profession, jobs are usually found through advertisements in the medical press. BMA members are advised to contact the International Department at the British Medical Association (BMA House, Tavistock Square, London WC1H 9JP; tel: 020 7387 4499, fax: 020 7383 6400, website: www.bma.org.uk) for information and advice on working abroad. Most intending emigrants would prefer to work in North America and Australasia, but opportunities are limited. Within the EU there is recognition of medical qualifications. Remuneration is highest in Germany and Denmark, followed by France, Belgium and Luxembourg, with the UK towards the bottom of the scale. But there is unlikely to be much of a 'brain drain' to Europe since there is already a surplus of doctors in training there and the profession is becoming particularly overcrowded in Italy and Scandinavia. Indeed the reverse is true with the National Health Service actively recruiting doctors and dentists from the Central and Eastern European countries that are now EU members.

The developing countries, by contrast, are in urgent need of doctors and nurses. The average doctor/patient ratio in these countries is about 1:10,000 compared with 1:750 in the UK; in some areas it is as high as 1:80,000, with rural areas being almost completely neglected. The International Health Exchange (1 Great George Street, London SW1P 3AA; tel: 020 7233 1100, fax: 020 7233 3590, e-mail: info@ihe.org.uk, website: www.ihe.org.uk) helps provide appropriately trained health personnel for programmes in countries in Africa, Asia, the Pacific, Eastern Europe, Latin America and other areas seeking assistance. It maintains a register of health workers for those actively seeking work in developing countries and areas requiring humanitarian aid.

International demand for UK nurses has been reduced by radical health service reforms in many countries, but opportunities still exist, particularly in the United States and the Middle East, for those with sound, post-registration experience and qualifications. The International Office of the Royal College of Nursing, 20 Cavendish Square, London W1G 0RN; tel: 020 7409 3333, website: www.rcn.org.uk provides overseas employment advice to its members, and overseas vacancies appear in weekly nursing journals such as *Nursing Standard*, on sale at newsagents.

In the UK, the Department for Business, Enterprise and Regulatory Reform (BERR) provides information on the mutual recognition of professional qualifications at degree level and above and has overall responsibility for the operation of the UK Certificate of Experience Scheme, which is run by the British Chambers of Commerce on behalf of BERR. The Department for Children, Schools and Families (DCSF) provides advice on qualifications below degree level.

Further information can be obtained from BERR at Bay 212, Kingsgate House, 66–74 Victoria Street, London SW1E 6SW; tel: 020 7215 5000, website: www.berr.gsi.gov.uk, and from DCSF at Room E4b, Moorfoot, Sheffield S1 4PQ; tel: 0870 000 2288, e-mail info@dfes.gsi.gov.uk for advice on international recognition of qualifications. Copies of the BERR/DCSF publication *Europe Open for Professions* are available from either organisation.

Information on the Certificate of Experience Scheme is available from the Certification Unit, British Chambers of Commerce, Westwood House, Westwood Business Park, Coventry CV4 8HS; tel: 024 7669 5688, website: www.britishchambers.org.uk.

Finally, one can get a direct comparison between any UK qualifications and those recognised in any EU country via the National Academic Recognition Information Centre (NARIC). However, you can only do this from abroad to the local jobcentre equivalent by asking to contact the local NARIC representative.

Business schools

For high-flyers, a possible route into the overseas job market is a course at one of the European business schools – either a short executive programme or a full-scale MBA. The latter course is in huge demand and is offered by a very large and ever-increasing number of schools worldwide, whether on a full-, part-time or distance-learning basis. The internet has also been adopted as a learning medium. However, one should weigh up its worth with care, given the effort, time and considerable expense involved. A book and directory of business schools approved by the Association of MBAs is the annual *AMBA Guide to Business Schools* (FT/Pitman).

Another possibility lies with the Open University Business School, which offers a range of six-month courses on a distance-learning basis: OUBS Customer Relations Centre, PO Box 625, Milton Keynes MK1 1TY; tel: 0845 366 6035, website: www.open.ac.uk/oubs.

The longest established European business school is INSEAD. Founded in 1959, today the school is widely recognised as one of the most influential business schools in the world. Its global scope and multicultural diversity make it the model for international management education. Located in Fontainebleau, France, INSEAD runs a 10-month MBA programme, a PhD programme and shorter executive development courses with a focus on general management in an international environment. Holders of the MBA can find jobs through the INSEAD Career Management Service. The emphasis is on international business management. Each year several hundred companies find that INSEAD is an excellent source for recruiting talented, multilingual and geographically mobile managers with high potential. Over one-third of graduates go on to start their own business sometime in their career. Students come from more than 50 countries with no single nationality dominating.

The majority of MBA students come as non-sponsored individuals. Various scholarships and loans are available. INSEAD is clearly a good investment for your future if you have the right background. Courses are taught in English but a fair knowledge of French is required. A third language is required in order to graduate and courses in German and Spanish are available. For further information contact INSEAD, MBA Admissions, Boulevard de Constance, F-77305 Fontainebleau Cedex; tel: +33 1 60 72 40 00, fax: +33 1 60 74 55 00, website: www.insead.edu.

Department for International Development

The Department for International Development (DfID) manages Britain's programme of aid to developing countries. The range of skills required under the programme is vast and constantly changing. Workers are drawn from a large number of backgrounds and professions such as agriculture, education and engineering.

The minimum requirement for most vacancies is usually a professional qualification and at least two to three years' relevant experience, including some in a developing country. A limited number of postgraduate study awards are also offered. Successful applicants are usually given assignments of up to two to three years as either a cooperation officer, employed by the DfID and 'on loan' to the overseas client government, or as a supplemented officer, under contract to the relevant government on local salary, with a supplement provided by the DfID to equal UK pay level.

Where the DfID needs immediate expert advice, consultants are used on appointments lasting from a few days to several months. Such assignments are open to both employed and self-employed specialists. The DfID also provides assistance to the United Nations and its specialist agencies (eg International Labour Office) in recruitment to field programmes, as well as the Junior Professional Officers Scheme.

For further information please write, enclosing a CV, to the Service and Resource Development Group, Room AH304, Department for International Development, Abercrombie House, Eaglesham Road, East Kilbride, Glasgow G75 8EA (tel: 01355 844000, fax: 01355 844099).

The British Council

The British Council (10 Spring Gardens, London SW1A 2BN; tel: 020 7930 8466, website: www.britishcouncil.org) promotes Britain abroad. It provides access to British ideas, talents and experience through education and training, books and periodicals, the English language, the arts, science and technology.

It is represented in 109 countries, 209 libraries and information centres and over 118 English language schools and has offices in 228 towns and cities. The Council provides an unrivalled network of contacts with government departments, universities, embassies, professional bodies and business and industry in Britain and overseas. The British Council is an independent and non-political organisation. In developing countries it has considerable responsibilities for the DfID in the field of educational aid, and in recent years it has become involved in the design and implementation of education projects funded by international lending agencies such as the World Bank.

The Council also acts as an agent for governments and other employers overseas in recruiting for contract teaching and educational advisory posts in ministries, universities, training colleges and secondary and primary schools. The Council usually guarantees the terms of such posts and sometimes subsidises them. In these appointments it works closely with the DfID. Teachers are also recruited on contract for the Council's network of English language schools.

Vacancies include teacher trainers, curriculum designers and British studies specialists for posts in projects or for direct placement with overseas institutions. Candidates must be professionally qualified and have appropriate experience.

Appointments are usually for one or two years initially and often renewable by agreement. Vacancies are advertised in *The Times Educational Supplement*, *The Guardian* and other journals as appropriate.

Teaching English as a Foreign Language

EFL teachers are in demand in both the private and public education sectors abroad. Public sector recruiting is usually done by the government concerned through the British Council; private recruitment varies from the highly reputable organisation (such as International House) to the distinctly dubious. Most EFL teachers have a degree and/or teaching qualification. A Cambridge CELTA qualification will also be required. Most employers will accept the Trinity College London Certificate (TESOL) and their Diploma as equivalents of CELTA and DELTA (website: www.tesolcourse.com). A four-week Cambridge Certificate in CELTA (Certificate in English Language Teaching to Adults) or the associated Diploma (DELTA) are available at International House in London and

Hastings (website: www.ihlondon.com), and at a number of other centres. The University of Cambridge Local Examinations Syndicate (tel: 01223 553311) can provide comprehensive lists of the centres running courses leading to these awards, worldwide. Alternatively, the website www.cambridgesol.org/centres/teach.htm has information on all training providers.

Bear the following points in mind when applying for an EFL post abroad:

- Will your travel expenses be paid? Some schools refund them on arrival or at the end of the contract.
- Is accommodation provided? If so, is it free or is the rent deducted from your salary? Is your salary sufficient to meet the deduction? If you find your own accommodation, are you helped to find it, especially if your knowledge of the local language is modest? Does the school lend you money to help pay the accommodation agency's fee and deposit? If the accommodation is provided, does it include hard or soft furnishing, and what should you bring with you?
- Contracts and work permits. Will you have a contract, how long for, and will the school obtain the permits to legalise your position in the country?
- Salary. Are you paid by the hour, week or month? If you are paid by the hour, is there a guaranteed minimum amount of teaching available for you? Do ensure that you can survive financially in the face of cancelled classes, bank strikes and numerous public holidays. Are there cost-of-living adjustments in countries with alarming inflation rates? Salaries are generally geared to local rates, but do make sure they are adequate. In sterling terms, one may earn a very low salary (in Rabat, for instance) yet enjoy a higher standard of living than a teacher earning double in Italy, or three times as much in Singapore.
- How many hours are you expected to teach? Be wary of employers who expect you to teach more than about 25 hours a week (remember you need additional time to prepare lessons). What paid leisure time do you expect? This is variable, but two weeks at both Easter and Christmas is fairly common.
- What type of student will you be teaching? Children or adults, those learning general English or English for special purposes (ESP)?

■ What levels will you be teaching and what course books will be used? Will there be a director of studies to help you over any initial difficulties and provide some form of in-service training?

A knowledge of the local language is an asset; in some situations, it is absolutely essential. Without it, one's social contacts are restricted to the English-speaking community which, in some areas, is virtually non-existent.

Locating the vacancies

1. International House recruits teachers only for its own affiliated schools, of which there are 100 in 26 countries. Vacancies elsewhere can be seen on the IH noticeboard in the Staffing Unit, 106 Piccadilly, London W1V 9FL (tel: 020 7518 6999, fax: 020 7518 6998, e-mail: info@ihlondon.co.uk, website: www.ihlondon.com). Other major reputable EFL institutes that anyone looking for a job would do well to try are:

   - Bell (www.bell-centres.com)
   - English First (www.englishfirst.com)
   - InLingua (www.inLingua.com)
   - Linguarama (www.linguarama.com)
   - Regent (www.regent.org.uk)
   - Saxon Court (www.saxoncourt.com)

2. Advertisements appear in publications such as *The Times Educational Supplement* (Fridays) and *The Guardian* (Tuesdays). Of course, many teachers are already overseas and can't get these newspapers. The international edition of *The Guardian* carries some advertisements, but many people look online: www.jobs.guardian.co.uk.

3. The British Council Teacher Recruitment Unit recruits EFL teachers for the British Council's Language Centres around the world. It can be contacted at 10 Spring Gardens, London SW1A 2BN (tel: 020 7389 4931, website: www.britishcouncil.org or via e-mail at teacher.vacancies@britishcouncil.org). British Council vacancies are also advertised in the press. The British Council Overseas Appointments Services recruits for posts funded directly by overseas employers. It can be contacted at Bridgewater House, 58 Whitworth Street, Manchester M1 6BB; tel: 0161 957 7383.

4. The Centre for British Teachers, CfBT Education Trust, 80 Queens Road, Reading, Berkshire RG1 4BS (tel: 0118 902 1000, fax: 0118 902 1434, e-mail: international@cfbt.com, website: www.cfbt.com) recruits teachers for English language teaching projects in Brunei, Oman and Turkey and educational specialists for consultancies on donor-funded projects in Eastern Europe, Africa, Asia and India.

5. If you want to learn more about English language teaching qualifications, Cactus Teachers are a helpful source of information (www.cactusteachers.com). They specialise in advice on CELTA and the Trinity College Certificate.

Voluntary work

Those who are technically skilled or professionally qualified and who would like to share their skills with developing countries could apply to VSO (Voluntary Service Overseas). VSO has over 1,750 skilled people working in 58 countries: in Africa, Asia, the Caribbean, Eastern Europe and the Pacific. Placements are in education, health, natural resources, technical trades, engineering, business, communications and social development. Volunteers are aged from 20 to 70, usually 23–60, with no dependent children.

Accommodation and a modest living allowance are provided by the local employer. Flights, insurance and other allowances are provided by VSO. Posts are generally for two years, but many volunteers stay longer.

Working as a VSO volunteer is very much a two-way process; volunteers often feel that they learn more from the society and culture they are involved with than they can possibly contribute. For further information contact The Enquiries Unit, VSO, 317 Putney Bridge Road, London SW15 2PN; tel: 020 8780 7200, website: www.vso.org.uk.

Checklist: Independent job opportunities

1. Research professional and national media for overseas jobs.
2. Investigate opportunities on the internet and place your CV with databanks on the web.
3. Check out the possibilities of turning a visitor's visa into a work permit before you look for a job on spec.
4. Contact your trade or professional associations for overseas vacancies and guidance on employment conditions and what to expect.
5. Consider taking a qualification, such as an MBA, in a foreign business school as a way to open doors overseas.
6. Examine the pay and conditions of language schools.
7. For teaching assignments, research opportunities through the British Council.
8. Have realistic expectations of short-term work such as au-pairing or working on a kibbutz, and ensure that all details are given in writing before departure.

2 Internationally Mobile Employees' Expectations

Employees of companies who are asked to transfer abroad by their employers are in a different category to overseas jobseekers. This chapter is intended to provide guidance to those in this situation before they make a decision, both on the terms of the remuneration package that they might look for and on the likely reasoning behind their employer's offer in the first place. Readers who are not working for a company now and do not intend to work in a corporate environment in the near future may prefer to omit this chapter and go forward to Part Two.

CATEGORIES OF OVERSEAS EMPLOYMENT

There are three situations in which your corporate employer might invite you to work abroad:

- on a short- or medium-term assignment, either as a commuter or as a temporary resident to provide management expertise or training (eg in the case of an acquisition) or support skills (eg for a technology transfer project);
- as a more permanent relocation to perform a particular local role, usually in a senior management position;
- as a part of a globally mobile executive cadre who move frequently from country to country in line with corporate strategy.

The third category of globe-trotting 'suits' is normally an organisational feature of multinational corporations or government foreign services. Their terms of overseas employment have evolved from experience of managing internationally mobile employees, often over decades, and are codified into HR policies and practices. If you are in this category, there will be very little or no scope for bargaining and you need to be sure that you are comfortable with company policies before you sign up for the long haul. The detail of this chapter may therefore be of interest only as an indicator of what other companies offer.

Before focusing on the remaining two categories of short- or medium-term assignments, let's take a look at the circumstances in which your company may want you to make a move.

WHEN AN OVERSEAS APPOINTMENT IS REQUIRED

The need to fill an appointment overseas with a manager or skilled employee, instead of appointing a local national, can apply equally to large multinational companies or smaller companies whose activities have extended from their home base into as little as one export market or one manufacturing unit abroad.

The circumstances of the organisation may extend from:

- companies engaged only in the export of goods and/or services abroad; to
- international companies with either overseas subsidiaries or loosely associated, autonomous operations in a few locations; to
- multinationals with operations in a number of countries in one or more regions, having common systems (in particular, IT and financial controls) and processes; to
- global corporations covering most developed and significant emerging economies, with universal branding, integrated marketing and manufacturing strategies and centrally controlled financial, corporate planning and human relations (HR) functions.

The continuing trend towards multinationalism reflects the ever-increasing economic interdependence of countries and the growing volume and diversity of transactions between them.

THE EMPLOYER'S PERSPECTIVE

HR strategy issues

For both the home company sending employees abroad and the host countries receiving them the key issues are clear; the transfer of skilled and experienced management or staff will inevitably disrupt the smooth running of their local businesses and almost certainly give rise to other staff deployments locally.

In the case of multinational and global corporations the issues are more complex. They will need to balance the interests of the home and host operations with the overriding group interests, which will include building and maintaining a cadre of well-motivated, experienced and effective internationally mobile employees. The development of a comprehensive HR policy for employees on international assignment is an essential element of their strategy without which the company is exposed to creating precedents and anomalies in terms of employment and remuneration packages that are likely to come back to haunt them when making fresh appointments or addressing employee grievances.

Even in smaller international or export-orientated companies there are some functions that are usually performed by expatriates from the headquarters country, such as start-ups in a new territory or training to deliver skills or transfer technology in local markets. In post-acquisition situations it is normal to import an expatriate general manager and financial controller for a time unless there are experienced, successful and adaptable local managers in post.

Whatever the size and scope of organisation, there are common areas for which each company individually defines its overseas assignment strategy:

- the business need;
- the extent to which local managers can be used;
- at what levels and in which functions expatriate managers will perform.

Profiling the candidate requirements for expatriate appointments

Inevitably, the different categories of assignment will demand different characteristics and qualities in the candidates from whom an appointee is selected.

Appointments of six months or less are commonest in the case of training local staff for skills or technology transfers, and appointees are usually drawn from mid-career managers or case-hardened older managers who are nearing the end of their careers. Aside from their technical prowess, successful appointees will need communication skills, patience and the willingness to tolerate unfamiliar living conditions for a limited period. Family considerations are unlikely to affect the decision to accept the appointment except in the case of single parents or those with dependants who cannot be left in the care of others.

Longer-term assignments of two to five years (some of which could result in localisation at the end of the appointment) are usually allotted to the same categories of manager, but the personal considerations are much more complex, involving the uprooting and relocation of families with all the attendant considerations that are the subject of this book. However, there may be significant long-term career issues that those who are offered expatriate employment will also need to address.

The trend towards so-called 'commuter' appointments where the internationally mobile employee travels from his or her base every week, usually within the same geographic region, has been growing. This is unlikely to be the employer's first choice for assignments to one location of more than six months, but may result from the unwillingness of the appointee's family to move. Generally, this is a bad solution. Although the considerable cost of moving a partner or family may be avoided, commuting imposes many strains on the employee, both socially and in work performance. It may also have a negative impact on peer relationships with local managers who resent the apparent privilege and dilution of involvement.

Career considerations for expatriate employees

In larger companies HR strategy may be focused on offering expatriate assignments to the most promising mid-career managers who are potential candidates in the future for top-level executive positions and for whom successful management experience abroad is a prerequisite. Turning down such an appointment for perfectly reasonable family considerations in such circumstances may mean accepting a ceiling to career advancement within the organisation.

It is important for you to recognise the implications if you are in that position and for you and your partner to talk through the consequences before taking a decision.

Senior managers nearing the end of their careers for whom an expatriate appointment may be the final assignment before retirement should focus on their position when the assignment comes to its end or is terminated prematurely. Pension benefits will be a prime consideration.

Many years ago, a friend of mine worked for a foreign multinational corporation in its London office. A British colleague in his late fifties who had worked for the company in South Africa in a senior position with a generous salary and benefits, he had returned to the UK subsidiary for his final five years' employment. Without the overseas benefits, his salary and prospective pension were no longer attractive against the higher cost of living in Britain. Realising that this was the HR policy for nationals of countries other than that of the parent company, my friend wisely chose to change his employer when offered a marketing appointment in the South African subsidiary.

Selection criteria

The most common competencies required for international managers are listed by Towers Perrin, the international executive employment consultants, as:

- cultural sensitivity;
- interpersonal skills;
- listening;
- flexibility/adaptability;
- ability to learn;
- personal ambiguity tolerance;
- emotional stability;
- technical competencies.

These qualities are perceived as of greater importance for longer-term assignments than technical skills and abilities by many employers.

In a survey several years ago, Towers Perrin also found that there was a close correlation, in descending order, of the perceived relative importance of the following characteristics between employers and employees:

- family flexibility;
- personal resilience;
- personality;
- cultural sensitivity;
- interpersonal skills;
- international experience;
- employability;
- language skills.

Except for language skills, rather higher percentages of employers than employees mentioned each factor.

TERMS OF EMPLOYMENT AND REMUNERATION

From the employee's perspective, the most important issues to be resolved with the employer are the contract and the remuneration package. The latter is, of course, a key element of the contract terms.

The employment contract: basic terms

Given that there is no job security in today's business world, it is normal for a contract of expatriate employment to specify:

- the length of the appointment;
- salary and benefits administration;
- a procedure for discussing repatriation in the final 6 to 12 months of the appointment;
- an extended period of notice in the event that a further appointment is not on offer.

Bearing in mind that some 40 per cent of international assignees are said to return early, it is important that your contract should include provision for the costs of repatriation in whatever circumstances are reasonably foreseeable and certainly in the event of dismissal.

You should also ensure that your expatriate employment contract includes provision for an annual appraisal, even if your compensation is not performance-related. The appraisal should include a review of personal performance against responsibilities and tasks defined in a job description attached to the contract and the joint setting of objectives for the next year. As well as being best practice among international employers, annual appraisals may be the only way of confirming your employer's view of your progress, successes and failures in the appointment when regular communication with home-country management colleagues and superiors throughout the year may be limited. Appraisals will also contribute to your peace of mind and effectiveness.

The compensation package

As already discussed, most international companies and all multinational or global corporations will have a detailed HR policy, which will include defined compensation packages for each grade of expatriate employee. These terms are unlikely to be negotiable, but you should be sure that you are comfortable with them.

If possible, you should ensure that, in addition to annual salary and cost of living reviews, your compensation package includes an equitable and fair element of reward incentive. You will find that there is a trend towards the inclusion of incentive rewards by many international companies.

If you are working for a smaller organisation, whose overseas appointments are occasional or sporadic, you may find that there is no established HR policy in place and that expatriate assignments are managed on an ad hoc basis. Therefore, there may be more scope for negotiation.

For example, in the case of an international company that has decided to develop a new manufacturing operation involving a transfer of technology from the home plant, the only practical course of action may be to send a senior factory manager for a period of two to three years to handle the start-up and to develop a local management capability. If an external appointment is not feasible because of the technology transfer and there are no more than one or two internal candidates, the company may find that its opportunistic decision to invest is matched by the preferred candidate's equally opportunistic demands for the most favourable reward package achievable. If you are the preferred candidate in such a situation, you may be wise not to push your demands to the limit. An exorbitant package, granted reluctantly, is likely to generate lingering resentment and you may find that there will be no commitment to a further appointment on your return.

CONCLUSION

Offers of an overseas appointment from an existing employer or resulting from recruitment always present an exciting challenge for you and your family. However favourable the terms may appear to be initially, be sure to work through the detailed checklist that follows before making an irrevocable decision.

Checklist: Employment conditions

If you have been offered employment abroad, bear in mind that you will incur a whole range of expenses which would not arise if you were employed here. It is vital to consider these expenses and to check whether your remuneration package covers them, either directly or in the form of fringe benefits.

If you are going to work for a reputable international company, it will probably have a standard reward package that includes the fringe benefits that it is prepared to offer. But if your employer is new to, or inexperienced in, the game of sending people to work abroad (especially if he or she is a native of the country to which you are going and therefore possibly not aware of expatriates' standards in such matters as housing) here are some of the factors you should look at in assessing how good the offer really is.

To help you arrive at realistic, up-to-date answers to the following questions, it is worth trying to talk to someone who has recently worked in the country to which you are thinking of going, as well as reading the relevant sections in this book.

1. **Family**
   (a) Is your employer going to help your partner find a job or to identify other opportunities such as further education or voluntary work?
   (b) If your employer is not able to help your partner find work, do they have a policy of reimbursing for loss of income?
   (c) Is your partner involved in the briefing sessions provided by your employer before departure?
   (d) Does your employer provide a support network for your partner?
   (e) Will your employer provide details of schools?

    (f) Do you have contacts provided by your employer to talk to before you move?

    (g) Is your employer going to meet the cost of travel out from the UK for your family as well as yourself?

2. Accommodation

    (a) Is your employer going to provide accommodation? If so:

         ☐ Of what standard?

         ☐ How soon will it be available after you arrive?

         ☐ Is it furnished or unfurnished? If furnished, what will be provided in the way of furniture?

    (b) If accommodation is not free, but there is a subsidy, is this assessed:

         ☐ As an absolute sum? In this case, is it realistic in the light of current prices? If not, is there any provision to adjust it?

         ☐ As a proportion of what you will actually have to pay?

    (c) Who is going to pay for utilities (gas, water, electricity, telephone)?

    (d) If there is no subsidy and accommodation is not free, are you sure your salary, however grand it sounds, is adequate? Do not accept the job unless you are sure about this.

    (e) Will the employer subsidise or pay for you and your family's hotel bills for a reasonable period until you find somewhere to live? Is the figure realistic in the light of local hotel prices?

3. Removal assistance

    (a) Will you be paid a disturbance allowance? Is it adequate to cover the cost of shipping (and, possibly, duty at the other end) for as many household and personal effects as you need? Will your eventual return to the UK as well as your departure be taken care of?

    (b) What arrangements will be made:

         ☐ To cover legal and other fees if you have to sell your UK home?

         ☐ To cover the difference, if you have to let your UK home while you are away, between the rental income and such outgoings as insurance, mortgage interest and agent's management? Will you be compensated for any legal expenses you incur, eg to get rid of an unsatisfactory tenant?

         ☐ To cover the cost of storing household effects?

4. Personal effects and domestic help

(a) Will you be paid a clothing allowance, bearing in mind that you will need a whole new wardrobe if you are going to a hot country? Will it cover just your clothes, or those of your family as well?

(b) Will your employer pay for or subsidise household items (eg air conditioning) that you will need in a hot climate and that are not included in an accommodation package?

(c) Will your employer provide/subsidise the cost of domestic servants? If not, is your salary adequate to pay for them yourself, if they are necessary and customary in the country and at the level at which you are being employed?

(d) Is a car going to be provided with the job – with or without driver?

(e) Will the employer pay for or subsidise club membership and/or entrance fees?

(f) Will you be paid an allowance for entertaining?

5. Leave entitlement

(a) If your children attend UK boarding schools, what arrangements are there for them to join you in the holidays? Will the employer pay for their air fares and if so will this be for every holiday or only some of them? If the latter, can you arrange for them to be looked after at Christmas or Easter?

(b) What arrangements are there for your own leaves? Does the employer provide return air fares to the UK or another country of your choice? Will these cover your family? And for how many holidays?

6. Personal finance

(a) Will the employer pay for/subsidise all or any additional insurance premiums you may incur? In some countries (eg Saudi Arabia) it is advisable to insure your servants. The cost of motor vehicle insurance may be inordinately high because of poor roads and low driving standards.

(b) If social security payments are higher than in the UK (eg in some EU countries), will your employer make up the difference?

(c)   Will the employer contribute to your medical expenses if free medical attention is not available or is inadequate?

7. **Salary**
   (a)   If your salary is expressed in sterling, would you be protected against loss of local buying power in case of devaluation? Equally, if your salary is in local currency, would it be adjusted for a rise in sterling against that currency?
   (b)   Is your salary in any way index-linked to the cost of living? How often are the effects of inflation taken into account in assessing and adjusting your current level of remuneration?
   (c)   If there are any restrictions on remittances, is your employer prepared to pay a proportion of your salary into a UK bank or that of some other country with a freely negotiable currency?

8. **Language**
   (a)   Will your employer contribute towards language teaching for you and/or your partner?

9. **Legal status**
   (a)   Is the legal status of your appointment clear? If you are held to be your employer's sole or principal representative, you may be personally liable in some countries for any obligations incurred, eg the payment of corporate taxes or social security contributions.
   (b)   Have all the terms of the job and the provisions of the remuneration package been confirmed in writing concerning the contract and conditions of employment subject to English law and, if not, do you or your advisers clearly understand how they should be interpreted should a dispute arise?

10. **Working for a foreign company**
    (a)   If the job is with a foreign company, particularly a locally based one rather than a multinational, there are a number of points that need special attention:
       ☐   Are the duties of the job clearly spelt out in writing in a contract of employment?
       ☐   Are the normal working hours laid down? How long will your journey to work be?

☐ Are all matters affecting pay, including when it is due and whether you will be paid for overtime, clear and in writing?

☐ If there is a bonus, are the conditions under which it is due unambiguous?

☐ Are there satisfactory arrangements for sick pay?

☐ Would there be any restriction on your changing jobs if you got a better offer from another employer or decided to leave? (This one obviously has to be handled with particular tact!)

☐ Do leave conditions clearly specify whether the leave is home or local? For the former, has the employer unambiguously declared the intention of paying your return air fare and that of your partner/family?

☐ Will legitimate expenses be paid in addition to salary?

(b) Have you taken any steps to check the bona fides of the prospective employer, eg through a Chamber of Commerce (the local/British Chambers of Commerce to be found in many main centres are often more obliging and better informed than commercial sections of British embassies), bank, trade association, or Dun & Bradstreet's Business Information Services?

11. **Personal protection**

(a) Is there a legal obligation on the employer in a high-risk country to continue to pay your salary if you are taken hostage?

(b) Will the employer offer you a special training course to cope with the risks involved in living in a very high-risk country?

(Much of the background information for this chapter was provided by Valerie Vardy and Mike Langley of Towers Perrin whose collaboration in previous editions the author gratefully acknowledges.)

3 | Expatriate Employees' Expectations

Stephen Gill, Stephen Gill Associates

THALES' WELL

An amusing story relates how Thales of Miletus, the 6th-century BC Greek philosopher, fell into a well one night while observing the night sky. He had been so intent in observing the heavens that he failed to watch where he was walking. The attractive servant-girl who answered his cries for help mockingly asked him how he expected to know anything about the stars when he didn't even know what was on earth under his own feet.

BACK TO THE FUTURE

I am often reminded of Thales' tumble when I hear of certain expatriate mishaps that occur. It is all too easy to focus on distant places and miss the obvious that is near at hand. Expatriates and their families have high expectations that often cause them to take their eye off the road ahead. Using Thales' fall as a metaphor, there are many potential pitfalls lying in wait for the expatriate, and the phrase 'overseas business trip' can take on a whole new meaning for the unwary. It is not possible to cover all the pitfalls here, but with Thales' fall firmly in mind we will start by looking at the area that for many is the expatriates' own bump back down to earth: repatriation.

Repatriation is the process of expatriates returning home from the international assignment, and it completes the cycle of the expatriation process. It is a commonly held belief that it will be a 'return to normal'. Unfortunately, repatriation is rarely an event that feels either easy or natural. On the contrary, it can also be made all the more difficult as repatriates themselves do not expect this 'reverse culture shock' to occur, as they are returning 'home' and are not prepared for it.

'Reverse culture shock' can be caused by the mismatching between the expatriates' high expectations prior to their return and the reality that they actually encounter after the return. Expatriates always expect they will hold similar, if not higher, hierarchical positions upon their return where there will be good opportunities to utilise the skills and knowledge that they acquired abroad.

In practice, it is often unrealistic and sometimes impossible to guarantee to expatriates the specific position they are expecting upon their return. Consequently, it is crucial for companies to be honest to expatriates in an attempt to try to minimise any readjustment difficulties when they return. Unfortunately, this seldom happens, as companies do not want to unsettle employees before the end of the assignment, and it is easy for companies to put it off until expatriates eventually arrive back.

A key ingredient for effective repatriation is to start early to make expatriates aware of all the possible outcomes from this career decision. Poor handling of repatriation may cause a high staff turnover problem or lower the expatriates' morale, thereby shrinking the potential expatriate pool if it is not handled properly.

One problem of repatriation is that many companies may not cherish the competencies and wisdom that their repatriates gained from their international assignments and may not take full advantage of the skills and knowledge that their employees acquired from working abroad. Expatriates' tolerance for ambiguity, magnified intercultural understanding and ability to relate effectively with people of different cultures are commonly not used by the expatriates' home organisations.

Disregarding the knowledge gained by expatriates could be counterproductive and expensive for the parent company, as considerable investment has been devoted to these members of staff. Therefore, for companies to ignore expatriates' gained knowledge could be viewed as poor management. It would be far better to provide chances for repatriates to utilise their skills, and that would encourage them to work more enthusiastically for the parent company.

However, companies that do not take advantage of the knowledge gained by their expatriates may unwittingly force repatriates to seek employment elsewhere, possibly with their competitors. As companies invest significant sums of money training expatriates, it would also be sensible to try to retain this knowledge and experience in the organisation. Therefore, potentially, the inability and failure to exploit the intellectual capital gained by expatriates could also be considered as another form of management failure, as the company cannot realise the full benefit from the expatriates' assignment.

For expatriates themselves, it can be naive to think that your high expectations will be truly fulfilled upon returning or that the company will be able to satisfy your new-found needs. If you are like most people, you will not be unaffected by the experience of working abroad, and you are probably not exactly the same person that you were when you left. It is difficult, when in the midst of change, to take stock and be aware of your own expectations, but if you really want to avoid some form of disappointment, looking ahead to repatriation and considering the options as early as possible is advisable.

FAMILY CONSIDERATIONS

Of course, looking so far ahead, right through to the conclusion of an assignment, is not so easy when expatriates are first faced with the prospect of an assignment. It is usual at this early stage to discuss the opportunity with a spouse to gain his or her support. The focus of the attention is usually the job itself and the working conditions for the expatriate. If it is an extended assignment it is possible that the spouse and family will have the opportunity to travel with the expatriate. Whether the family accompanies the expatriate or is left behind, the importance of the role that it plays in international assignments should be recognised.

Family-related issues often have important influences upon expatriates' own adjustment processes and their ability to perform effectively on the assignment. Challenges regarding the children, language and the adjustment of spouses are likely to heighten the expatriates' levels of stress and uncertainty. Those expatriates whose family members are having difficulties adjusting are likely to feel responsible for their unhappiness, whereas contented families are obviously more likely to provide support.

The family generally experiences a more difficult adjustment process than the expatriates, as expatriates still feel the familiarity of the work. Families actually experience 'excessive culture shock' in many circumstances. This may lead to families facing challenges such as loss of self-esteem, lack of contact with friends and family, and social and cultural ostracism; disruption of children's education is also a contributing factor.

Therefore, a vital factor in successful expatriation is the ability of the expatriate and the trailing spouse and family to adjust to an unfamiliar foreign culture. It is a realistic claim that one of the main reasons for the premature return of expatriates is the inability of their spouses to adapt to the foreign environment and culture. Unfortunately, family circumstances are still the least likely to be considered before going on an assignment, which is a shame, as no organisations should underestimate the role that the expatriates' families play.

It seems that, whilst organisations acknowledge that it could be vital to the success of expatriate assignments that they formulate strategies to include families as much as the expatriates, perhaps they feel that they would be interfering in expatriates' personal lives to go so far as to include the families in preparation and adjustment programmes. This reluctance to involve partners earlier may in fact prevent organisations from choosing the most suitable couples, which would reduce the risk of expatriate failure.

Fortunately, not all companies are the same, and organisational concern about expatriate performance is increasing. It is now more widely understood that the parent company constitutes the initial source of support and provides benefits and services prior to arrival and that, once the expatriates are in the foreign country, these will affect expatriates' quality of life and work there.

Such support and services include financial benefits to maintain the standard of living to which expatriates are accustomed in the home country, cross-cultural training, assistance in housing relocation, membership of clubs in the foreign country, rest and relaxation, vacation leave, and assistance with schooling for children, as well as maintaining communication with the expatriates to ease anxieties.

Social support from a host country national can help family members' adjustment by providing feedback on the appropriate behaviour, and this can serve to lessen uncertainty regarding the local culture and thus facilitate a spouse's adjustment. To assist in this, a number of employers may help to provide spouses with a host country mentor to carry out these functions and help trailing spouses to establish networks with host country nationals.

Some companies are now providing expatriates with pre-departure and post-arrival training to help them and their families to adapt more successfully to the foreign culture. Thus the purpose of the training is to reduce the amount of culture shock that the expatriates or their families encounter by familiarising them with the host country. Training also helps to increase the expatriates' commitment to the parent organisation, perhaps also leading to higher performance.

In addition, training can make the change easier for people to accept because it reduces the fear and uncertainty that accompany many changes. Once employees have been selected for expatriate positions, pre-departure training is considered to be the next necessary step in attempting to ensure they can work effectively and successfully abroad.

Some companies go further and help expatriate family members adjust to the foreign environment by either providing job opportunities to the spouses or encouraging them to participate directly in the expatriation process to enhance the likelihood of success. Such support also extends to children, where it is recognised that it should focus more on language skills prior to expatriation and on continuing learning in the host country to help increase the children's cultural sensitivity and teach them to avoid premature judgement of the culture.

Everyone involved in an expatriate assignment wants it to be a success, but unfortunately it is often the task that receives all the focus whilst many elements that contribute to the success or failure are overlooked until they become a problem. Working abroad is an important step for anyone. If you are to avoid losing your footing as Thales did, beware the pitfalls that lie ahead.

Part Two:

Managing Personal Finance

4 Domicile and Residence

When leaving the UK on secondment you must consider the impact on your residence and domicile status, as this will dictate how you are treated for taxation purposes during your assignment. With effect from 5 April 2008, non-UK-domiciled persons working in the UK are severely penalised. If you are thinking of staying abroad at the end of an assignment and commuting to the UK to work, you should review the consequences carefully.

THE CONCEPTS

Domicile is a complex legal issue, but normally you are domiciled in the country in which you have your permanent home. The place of domicile is where you intend to reside indefinitely and the country to which you ultimately intend to return.

A domicile of origin is usually inherited from your father at birth (or from your mother, if either your parents did not marry or your father died before you were of legal age). Establishing a new domicile of choice is extremely difficult, and in the case of someone with a domicile in the UK is only achieved by emigrating permanently to another country with no intention of returning to the UK and by severing all ties with the UK.

Your residence status for tax purposes is determined by the facts and your intentions and is therefore likely to be affected by an overseas assignment. UK tax law distinguishes between 'residence' and 'ordinary residence'. Whereas residence is based on UK physical presence in each tax year, ordinary residence equates broadly to habitual residence and takes into account the individual's intentions and UK presence over the short and medium term.

UK nationals leaving the UK for an assignment abroad will remain UK resident for tax purposes unless the overseas employment contract and the absence abroad cover at least one complete UK tax year (6 April to 5 April). In addition, the individual's visits to the UK must not exceed 183 days in total in any one tax year or an average of 91 or more days per tax year averaged over a maximum of four years.

When working abroad you should always consider the host country's definition of residence and domicile. Most countries without a legal system inherited from the UK do not have the concept of 'domicile' as understood in the UK and may base domicile on factors such as the intention to reside long-term. Other countries may use the word 'domicile' or its equivalent in their language to mean no more than a place of abode.

Having a UK domicile and UK-resident status does not preclude you from becoming a resident or domiciliary of the host country under its domestic tax law. In these circumstances, double taxation may arise and complicate the situation.

THE IMPACT ON UK TAXATION

The expatriate who does not break UK residence

If you are domiciled in the UK and remain resident and ordinarily resident during your assignment, your liability to UK tax on your worldwide employment and investment income, capital gains and assets will continue. Capital gains tax and inheritance tax will be chargeable irrespective of the location of the relevant assets. Explained below is the way that the correct use of foreign tax credits, double tax treaties and effective planning can prevent double taxation and mitigate your overall exposure to taxation.

One advantage of remaining UK resident is that you remain eligible to contribute to tax-efficient investments like ISAs. However, being non-resident does not always result in losing your right to make tax-deductible pension contributions (see below).

The non-UK resident expatriate

A non-UK resident is taxable in the UK only on employment income relating to duties performed in the UK. If these UK duties are, however, merely incidental to the overseas duties (eg receiving instructions, reporting on progress, or up to 91 days each year of training during which no productive work is done), the earnings should not be liable to UK income tax.

Nevertheless, you may still be liable to UK income tax on employment income received while non-resident. This arises in the case of bonuses, termination payments and the exercise of unapproved stock options (if you were UK resident when the option was granted or the grant relates to UK duties). As these items are earned over a period of time, HM Revenue and Customs (HMRC) in the UK may tax the proportion of the income that relates to the period of UK residence and to any non-incidental duties performed in the UK when non-resident.

If you are not UK resident, income from your foreign investments is outside the scope of UK income tax. Even if you are UK resident, it will not be chargeable to UK tax if you are not UK domiciled and you do not bring any of the income into the UK. Income from UK investments such as rental income from UK property, dividends on UK shareholdings and interest on UK accounts will continue to be liable to UK income tax.

Subject to any legislative changes that may be introduced in the 2008 Finance Act, capital gains tax cannot normally be avoided by being non-UK resident at the time the gain arises. Individuals who have been resident or ordinarily resident in the UK during any part of four out of the previous seven tax years and leave the UK may be liable to capital gains tax in the year of their return on any gains made during their absence. A UK absence of five complete tax years or more, however, negates this rule. The rule also usually only applies to assets already held by the individual when he or she leaves the UK (so that gains on assets that are both acquired and disposed of during a shorter non-resident period can be tax-free). Note that the terms of a double tax treaty between the UK and the new country of residence may also override the UK charge. Specific professional advice should be sought if you might dispose of assets during your UK absence.

You should note that, subject to certain conditions, capital gains tax is not usually chargeable on the sale of your UK property if it has been your only or main residence. Advice should be obtained to ensure that maximum advantage is taken of this generous relief.

The assets of a UK domiciliary may be charged to UK inheritance tax on death or earlier transfer, irrespective of their location and the residence status of the individual. Individuals who are not UK domiciled should note the 'deemed domicile' provisions, which impose UK inheritance tax on their worldwide assets if they have been UK resident for 17 out of the last 20 tax years. Specialist advice should always be obtained before making any gifts, and an appropriate will is essential for all expatriates.

If you remain employed by the UK company or a group company while working abroad, you can continue to contribute, and to have employer contributions made, to your UK occupational pension scheme. This can normally continue for 20 years or longer with HMRC approval and provided that you intend to return to work in the UK. The non-UK consequences of maintaining a UK pension scheme should always be considered, as the employer contributions may be taxable in your host country.

It is also possible to continue making contributions to a personal pension plan (including one that is funded by your employer) for up to five UK tax years of non-residence, provided that certain conditions are met. Income tax relief will be given at source on your personal contributions at the basic rate (currently 22 per cent but reducing to 20 per cent from April 2008) even if you do not have any UK-taxable income.

When you are non-resident in the UK, you will no longer be eligible to take out new tax-efficient investment schemes (such as ISAs) or to contribute to them, although you can continue to retain existing schemes. Tax relief on life assurance premiums on pre-March 1983 policies is also forfeited for your period of non-residence.

YOUR EMPLOYMENT PACKAGE

Employers have many options when considering how to structure an expatriate remuneration package. The decision is based on many factors, of which tax is just one. Set out below are the three main categories of expatriate package, and the type of expatriate to whom they are usually offered.

Tax equalisation

The basic principle of equalisation is that the expatriate continues to pay the same amount of tax as would have been paid if he or she had continued working in the home country (on the home country package). Social security contributions may also be included in this calculation. The employer deducts an amount equal to the normal home country tax (hypothetical tax) from the employee's salary and then assumes responsibility for paying the individual's actual tax liability, wherever it arises.

The actual tax paid on behalf of the employee by the employer is, in itself, a taxable payment and must be grossed up. The employer meets any additional liability to tax in excess of the hypothetical tax, but equally will retain any tax savings that arise during the assignment. For example, an employer settling tax on behalf of an employee liable at 40 per cent actually has to pay UK tax at 100/40 (a 67 per cent effective rate), but is able to use the hypothetical tax withheld from the individual to fund this. There may also be tax savings from tax breaks in the home and host countries as a result of the assignment. Companies with large expatriate populations tend to use this method because it encourages mobility, since it provides expatriates with more certainty about their take-home pay.

Tax protection

This method can be less expensive for the employer, but can be more difficult to administer. The principle is that expatriates will pay no more tax than they would have done had they remained working in the home country. No hypothetical tax is withheld by the employer. Instead the individual pays the actual home and host country tax up to the amount of the normal home country tax liability. If the actual overall tax liability is higher, the employer will pay the excess. If there is a saving by comparison to the normal home country liability, the expatriate keeps it. Sometimes only part of the expatriate's earnings is tax protected, for example foreign accommodation costs paid by the company.

This method is often used by companies sending expatriates to countries with lower tax rates than the home country. It can discourage mobility, as it provides a financial incentive for assignees to move to low-tax countries from high-tax countries and to stay there.

Laissez-faire

This method does not involve the employer at all (apart from any responsibilities like employer's social security contributions). The individual is simply responsible for his or her own tax liability in the home and host countries. This may be beneficial if the overall tax rates on assignment are lower than the normal home country rates.

This method is often applied where the expatriate has requested the assignment, to career development assignments by companies with little experience of international assignments, and by companies continually sending expatriates to countries that have no income tax or very low tax rates.

PLANNING POINTS

Timing

As explained above, UK non-residence is normally only achieved where a full-time overseas employment and the employee's UK absence cover a complete UK tax year. Thus, if the assignment was planned to begin on 20 April, you should consider bringing forward the date that the overseas employment commences and the UK departure date, so that they fall before 6 April.

There are tax reliefs for certain overseas assignments of two years or less, the details of which are set out below. HMRC will reject claims to relief from the date when there is a clear intention for the assignment to last more than two years or where the employee is under an employment contract with the company in the host location. Indicators such as work permits, social security certificates and assignment letters will be taken into account.

An overseas assignment that results in the individual being present in the host country for less than 184 days and during which he or she remains resident in the home country may provide the opportunity to avoid an income tax liability in the host country under the terms of a double taxation treaty. Remember that in most countries the tax year is the calendar year, so there may be scope for some planning on this point, although some tax treaties count the individual's days on a different basis to the tax year (see below).

If you are about to be granted share options, you should consider carefully whether it is preferable for you to be granted them before or after your UK departure. The option gains are likely to be taxable in either the home or host country (if not both) and your marginal tax rates in each country should be considered.

Non-contractual payments on termination of employment may be wholly or partly exempt from UK tax, if the employment involved periods of foreign service. You should seek advice if you receive such a payment, as the UK tax savings can be considerable but there may also be a foreign tax charge.

Avoiding double taxation

The UK has double tax treaties with numerous countries, which try to prevent double taxation of individual income and gains. There are also a few treaties that cover potential double taxation of capital assets. Although treaties vary and they should be examined in detail in every case, the rules for exemption of earnings from tax in the host country are normally:

- You must be UK resident under the definition in the treaty.
- You should not be present in the host country for more than 183 days (in the fiscal year, the calendar year or any 12-month period, depending on the treaty).
- You must remain employed by a business that is resident in the UK and that is not resident in the host country.
- The costs of your assignment must not be borne by a branch or permanent establishment of your employer in the host country (or, in some countries, by a subsidiary or parent company).

In some circumstances, double taxation is unavoidable. In these cases, the UK HMRC will normally reduce the UK tax by the foreign taxes paid on the double-taxed earnings, up to the amount of the UK tax otherwise payable.

Expatriate reliefs and allowances

Where an expatriate does not break UK residence, there are a number of tax reliefs that should not be overlooked. These include the following:

- For assignments that are not expected to exceed two years, a tax deduction can normally be claimed in respect of your additional living costs on the basis that you are working away from your normal workplace. The deduction can include the cost of the overseas accommodation and related costs, meals, travel and subsistence (but you must be prepared to produce receipts or other documentation to support your claim). Equally, if the employer reimburses these costs, HMRC will not normally tax them if they meet the conditions for the deduction. Alternatively, a tax-free, flat-rate allowance of £10 per night is available to cover incidental expenses when working abroad.

- For longer-term assignments, the following reimbursed expenses are normally not taxable in the UK:
  - qualifying relocation costs of up to £8,000, when leaving the UK and on returning from the assignment;
  - outbound and return travel costs for you and your family (including children under 18 at the start of the outward journey);
  - home leave travel for certain family members.
- All individuals who are Commonwealth or EEA nationals are entitled to a personal allowance that is deductible from their income taxable in the UK, as are nationals of certain other countries with which the UK has a double tax treaty regardless of whether they are resident or non-resident in the UK. This allowance is £5,435 for the 2008/09 UK tax year.

Tax on investments

If you are going to become non-UK resident, you may consider moving your UK investments offshore prior to your departure. This can potentially avoid UK tax on income arising from those investments while you are on assignment (but note that there may be a tax charge in the host country).

Before you return to the UK, you should close down all interest-bearing overseas bank accounts before the date on which you resume UK residence, in order to avoid UK income tax on the interest credited while you are non-resident. If you close the accounts after you have resumed UK residence, the interest credited from the date UK residence resumed will be taxable in the UK.

Finally, you should be aware that the host country may tax your investment income during your assignment, in particular where the local rules tax residents on their worldwide income and gains.

CONCLUSION

The key issue in expatriate taxation is to plan in advance. You might be able to save yourself a substantial amount of tax by merely adjusting the terms of your assignment package, but this must be weighed up against the personal and commercial needs of your secondment.

Checklist: Tax aspects of leaving the UK

1. Plan ahead. Consult a tax professional to ensure that your remuneration package and investment portfolio have been structured tax-efficiently, from both a UK and host country perspective. Ideally, you should try to meet a UK adviser before you leave the UK, and a host country adviser on arrival in the new location.
2. Inform HMRC. File a UK HMRC departure form P85. Take care with the wording of your answers on this document, as it will form the basis of the HMRC's evaluation of your residence status during your assignment (and may therefore affect the amount of tax you will pay). If you intend to let your UK property while you are non-UK resident, you should complete a non-resident landlord form NRL1 so that your rent can be received without the requirement for the tenant or agent to withhold tax from the rent. Remember, you may be required to file arrival forms and annual documentation in the host country.
3. Inform your bank, building society and insurer. Even if you do not expect your UK bank interest to exceed your tax-free personal allowance, if you will be not ordinarily resident in the UK you can receive bank interest gross while overseas (ask for the form at the bank or building society). This will save you from having to file a tax return to obtain any refund of withholding tax. If you believe your UK-source income will exceed your tax-free personal allowance, you may wish to set up an offshore bank account so that your bank interest is not liable to UK tax. You should advise your insurer that you will be living and working abroad, as this may affect the cover under your life and household policies.
4. Notify your payroll department. In many cases, you will need to stay on the UK payroll in order to continue making UK pension and UK National Insurance (social security) contributions. If you expect to become non-UK resident, apply to HMRC for an NT (no tax) code to prevent withholding of tax (PAYE) from your salary. If

you are going to remain UK resident and expect to pay foreign tax on your earnings, you should apply for the foreign tax to be included in your PAYE code number or set against your UK PAYE by your payroll department, to avoid double tax during the year.

5. Inform your pension provider. Check whether you remain eligible to make tax-deductible contributions to your pension scheme.

6. File a UK tax return. The tax reliefs and allowances available to expatriate assignees must be claimed on your UK tax return. A repayment of UK tax may be due, as personal allowances are given in full for each tax year, even if you are only UK resident for part of the year.

7. Register in your host country. Do this on arrival and take appropriate professional advice to avoid the risk of large and unexpected tax bills at the end of the tax year.

Checklist: Tax aspects of returning to the UK

1. Plan ahead. Seek advice if you have made capital gains, received large payments such as termination payments, or have a complex investment portfolio. If you are considering exercising stock options you should seek advice on timing issues.

2. Close offshore accounts. To prevent the UK from taxing the accrued interest, ideally you should close the accounts in the tax year before the year in which you return to the UK.

3. Deregister with the host country. Ensure you have informed the appropriate authorities of your departure, to prevent any attempt to dispute your actual date of departure.

4. Register with HMRC. File an arrival form P86. This form will not only dictate your tax treatment from the date of your UK return date, but also validate your tax treatment during your absence.

5 Banking, Financial Planning and Asset Management

For most people, working abroad means a rise in income. For those in countries with a low rate of income tax, or, as is the case in some countries in the Middle East, without income tax, it may be the first chance they have had to accumulate a substantial amount of money, and this may indeed be the whole object of the exercise. Expatriates are therefore an obvious target for firms and individuals offering financial advice on such matters as tax, mortgages, insurance schemes, school fee funding, income building plans and stock and 'alternative' investments. Most of them are honest, but some are better than others, either in choosing investments wisely or in finding schemes that are most appropriate to the needs and circumstances of their client, or both. At any rate the expatriate with money to spend is nowadays faced with a wide variety of choices, ranging from enterprising local traders proffering allegedly valuable antiques, and fly-by-night operators selling real estate in inaccessible tropical swamps, to serious financial advisers and consultants. The internet might also help independently minded investors in remote locations, and provides another source of advice.

UK expatriates live all over the world, 95 per cent of them in Australia, Hong Kong, Canada, Spain, South Africa, New Zealand, Germany, Ireland, France, the United States, the UAE, Argentina, Cyprus, Italy and The Netherlands. Some people will love their

new environment and may stay on for longer than originally anticipated. Some may loathe it and can't wait to get back.

When moving to a country that has a totally different culture and way of life you will need to respect and adhere to differing traditions and customs. Not only will the language be 'alien' but so too will be the culture and the general way of life. Before you 'up sticks' you need to spend some time in methodical planning. After all, the key to any successful move is to be well prepared and organised. Limiting potential problems or issues will help you to settle in and adjust quickly to your new 'homeland'.

A good starting point is to research your destination so you know what to expect. There may be a 'British' or 'Expatriate' community where you are moving to, which will help you to understand what help and support is available to you and your family. Assistance may also be available from your employer or more widespread support organisations.

OFFSHORE BANKING SERVICES

Lloyds TSB International – meeting the needs of expats and global commuters

With the rise of intercontinental living and working, an ever-increasing number of people are faced with the challenges of managing their finances on a global scale. Lloyds TSB International can provide a seamless resource for banking internationally offering customers access to a wide range of financial products and services, including international bank accounts, savings accounts, mortgages and loans.

International accounts are offered in sterling, the US dollar and the euro, and are available with globally accepted debit cards and a sterling chequebook to manage day-to-day finances while abroad. The first three months' banking is subscription fee free, with a monthly fee of £7.50/$7.50/€7.50 thereafter. Accounts can be opened with just £100/$100/€100, boasting the lowest minimum balance and subscription fee in the marketplace. Additionally, dedicated international banking advisers can provide introductions to a tax expert who can advise on international tax issues tailored to individual needs.

Other benefits of the international account, designed to fit with an international lifestyle, include:

- choice of accounts in three currencies – sterling, the US dollar and the euro;
- debit cards in all three currencies;
- 24/7 telephone and internet banking;
- Sentinel® International – wherever you are in the world, you can have all your credit and debit cards stopped, and replacements issued, with just one call;
- discounts on health and travel insurance;
- concierge service – use this service to book tickets for special events around the world, send gifts, even to manage your diary and receive reminders, and much more;
- a quarterly magazine, *Shoreline*.

The international mortgage service is designed to take the worry of securing finance away from you so that you can enjoy the benefits of owning your dream home abroad. So successful is this service that it has been awarded the 'Best Overseas Mortgage Lender' by *Your Mortgage* and *Mortgage Solutions* magazines.

This service is geared towards investors globally purchasing a holiday home abroad or an overseas property for investment purposes or building up a portfolio of properties abroad. Residential properties can be financed in Great Britain, Spain, France, Portugal, Dubai, New Zealand, Hong Kong and Singapore, as well as selected locations in Australia, Canada and the United States. Lending limits are normally five times individual or joint gross (basic) income, and are available in all major currencies. With no early repayment fee, and a free currency switching option allowing two free switches per calendar year, you can't afford to leave home without it!

For further information on the international account, international mortgage service or any other international products please contact the team of international banking advisers on +44 (0)1624 638000 or visit www.lloydstsb-offshore.com/workingabroad.

FOREIGN CURRENCY

If you're intending to work overseas it's important that you don't forget about the impact that foreign exchange can have on your finances, both before you go and once you arrive. Exchange rates are constantly moving and as a result can have a big impact on the amount of money you have to start your new life abroad.

Foreign currency specialists, such as No1currency, remove all the worries and complications associated with moving your finances and provide you with:

- bank-beating exchange rates;
- no commission charges;
- guidance and support;
- a fast, efficient, secure service.

Once you have moved, a foreign exchange specialist like No1currency can also help with regular overseas payments. If you have an income that you would like to be transferred on a regular basis, they can arrange to have the transactions processed on specific dates set by you. It is also possible to secure a rate for a fixed period of time, thus ensuring that you are not exposed to negative foreign exchange rate movements.

When it comes to transferring hard-earned assets, everyone wants to get the best rate possible. The choice usually comes down to either your high street bank or a foreign currency specialist such as No1currency. But what exactly is the difference?

Steve Smyth is married with a 10-year-old daughter. He was working in the RAF and was offered a senior position that involved emigrating to New Zealand:

As soon as we started planning the move last March, I began to consider the financial implications. I visited NZ in July and a former RAF colleague there gave me advice on a range of brokers, and said that, in his view, No1currency were the best.

Establishing a base involved lots of financial planning: I had to set up a new house, buy a car and transfer my family's belongings. No1currency provided an absolutely top-class personal service.

Overall, No1currency saved me a significant amount of money, especially in comparison with the high street banks, in terms of charges and foreign exchange rates. The best financial advice I can offer anyone considering emigrating is to look at the market and remember that you do have an alternative to the high street banks.

To find out how a foreign exchange specialist can benefit you, you can visit No1currency online at www.No1currency.com or speak directly to a specialist on 0800 237 037.

ALTERNATIVES FOR INVESTING SURPLUS INCOME

There are really only three types of objectives in investment: growth, income, and growth with income. The choice of one main objective usually involves some sacrifice in regard to the other. A high degree of capital appreciation generally implies a lower level of income and vice versa. Growth with income is an ideal, but generally it means some growth with some income, not a maximisation of both. Ultimately, the objective is the preservation of capital in bad times and the increase of wealth in good ones, but your adviser cannot perform miracles. If he or she is lucky enough to catch the market in an upward phase, as in the case of the recent equities 'bull' market, he or she may be able to show quick results, but normally investment is a process that pays off over a longer period and through the course of varying market cycles.

The prolonged 'bear' market in equities, which preceded the last bull market, exposed the fallibility of fund managers. Few foresaw the length or depth of the decline in equity prices, or reacted by switching their clients' funds into stable fixed-interest securities before heavy losses were incurred. Watch out now for history repeating itself.

INVESTMENT THROUGH UK OR OFFSHORE MANAGED FUNDS

There are many investment opportunities in the offshore fund markets, from specialised funds in individual countries to international ones spread across many industries. There are equally many ways of investing: regular investments, lump-sum purchase of units, periodic and irregular investments. It is also possible to invest in commodity markets and there are specialists trading in gold, silver, diamonds, sapphires and metals generally. Another innovation is the currency fund referred to earlier, which regulates holdings of foreign exchange and aims to predict fluctuations in exchange rates.

Your consultant should be able not only to inform you of the various schemes available, but also to advise on the degree of risk, the quality of management available and the combination of investments most likely to achieve your aims.

For those who prefer the safety of banks or building society deposits, there is now a concession to non-residents – interest is paid without tax being deducted at source. However, you will have to inform your bank about your non-resident status. A building society may also require you to open a separate, non-resident account.

You may still be assessed for income tax on any interest earned in the year of your return to the UK. For this reason, there are a number of advantages in taking up the facilities that UK banks offer non-residents to open an account in one of the established tax havens, notably the Channel Islands and the Isle of Man.

In all cases, though, there are important tax considerations before you return to the UK. You should discuss these with your adviser at least six months before then, so that the necessary plans can be drawn up in light of the current and pending taxation regime.

SCHOOL FEES PLANNING

There are many schemes available for school fees planning. These schemes aim to provide you with a tax-free income at a specified date for a predetermined length of time. They need not necessarily be used for educational purposes, and some readers may feel that if the employer is paying school fees, as is often the case, there is no need to take out such a policy. However, parents should bear in mind that it is highly advisable not to interrupt children's education, and taking out such a policy would obviously be a good way of ensuring that your child could go on with his or her education at the same school, even if your employment with that employer ended.

BASIC PLANNING POINTS

There are a number of basic planning points for expatriates to bear in mind, whatever their nationality of origin or place of work.

Two tax regimes

Usually there will be two tax regimes to consider: the home tax regime and the host tax regime. Almost invariably these will operate in different ways. The interaction between the two can be complex, but it is a vital part of sound financial planning. Advice based on only the host or home country's rules is best avoided; what works in the UK may not work over there and vice versa. Therefore, potential British expats should read and understand the advice provided in Chapter 4 relating to the UK taxation aspects of working abroad and review carefully the summary of the taxation regime to which they plan to transfer (contained on the website for which you have a password).

Fundamentals that do not change

While tax rules will vary from country to country, many of the fundamentals of financial planning apply across the globe. For example, it will always make sense to hold a rainy-day cash reserve in a readily accessible deposit account. For expatriates, that might mean two cash reserves – one in their host currency and one in their home currency.

While being an expatriate may offer tax advantages, tax must not become the only reason for doing something. So, for example, investment decisions should firstly be made on investment grounds, with tax then being considered only in terms of the structuring of the investment, eg whether the chosen investment fund is set up onshore or offshore.

Regular professional reviews are vital

All financial plans must be reviewed regularly. Laws can change with great speed, rendering last year's tax-efficient plan this year's no-go area. The UK has seen plenty of examples of this in recent years, some of which have had a direct impact on expatriates. It is particularly important to review plans a year or so before returning home – if sufficient advance warning is available.

If in doubt, the expatriate should always seek professional advice. The combination of different legal and tax regimes can make what would be a simple matter for the ordinary UK employee subject to UK tax highly complex for the expatriate counterpart. As a general rule, only the larger financial and accountancy firms will possess the necessary expertise.

PLANNING FOR DEPARTURE FROM THE UK

The sooner the would-be expatriate takes professional advice on financial planning the better. There will usually be a number of decisions to be made and changes to be undertaken, all of which are best not handled hastily. These are covered in the following sections.

Dealing with the home

As a general rule, leaving a property empty while overseas is best avoided, as there will always be a concern about vandalism or occupation by squatters. From a financial planning viewpoint, an empty property is a poor use of capital. It will yield no income but continue to generate costs such as general maintenance and, probably, mortgage interest. If the home will not be occupied by family members while the employee is working overseas, the real choice is whether it should be sold or rented out.

The case for selling is that it removes the problem of looking after a property from a distance and clears an outstanding mortgage debt. Some people will prefer to sell rather than have strangers (ie tenants) in their home. Selling property will also produce a lump sum to invest, but this may create its own problems in terms of investment risk, as the money will normally be earmarked for future property purchase on return to the UK.

Conversely, the major advantage of renting out property is that it allows the expatriate to retain a foothold in the UK residential property market. There are plenty of cautionary tales of expatriates who sold up only to find that, on their return several years later, they could not afford to buy the equivalent of their former property because of price increases during their absence. The case for letting and insuring your house while you are away and some explanation on how to do this with professional advice are presented later in this chapter.

Pension benefits

In this area it is important to determine how the expatriate's employment will be structured. Will he or she be employed by the UK employer or will the contract of employment be moved to an overseas employer, possibly a subsidiary?

If the expatriate remains employed by the UK company, then the employee can remain in that employer's occupational pension scheme unless the transfer abroad is permanent. An expatriate working for an overseas employer may retain membership of his or her UK pension scheme, subject to a number of conditions specified by HMRC. The most notable of these is that the pension entitlement must be based on the remuneration that would have applied had the employment been in the UK.

Expatriates with personal pensions are less favourably treated. If they are not resident for tax purposes, then neither they nor their employer can make personal pension contributions in respect of their overseas earnings. This could mean that pension-linked life cover has to be cancelled. Any remuneration package for the expatriate will need to take account of the pension position in terms of the impact on benefit entitlement and any foreign tax liabilities that might arise.

Ancillary employee benefits

Alongside pension rights, there will also be other benefit entitlements that need to be addressed as part of the expatriate's financial planning. The most significant of these is adequate private medical insurance, and the provision of expatriate medical cover is discussed in detail in Chapter 9. Permanent health insurance (income protection cover) should also be reviewed in the context of overseas employment.

Existing investments

As a broad rule, existing investments do not need to be disturbed ahead of departure from the UK, other than as part of normal financial planning:

- ISAs can continue to be held by non-UK residents with unchanged tax advantages.

- Unit trusts, shares and life insurance policies can all be retained. Although these may give rise to a UK tax liability (at no more than the basic rate), for a non-UK resident what limited potential tax savings are available by moving offshore would probably be offset by the costs of sale and reinvestment.
- Deposit accounts are an exception to the general rule. A non-UK resident can request to receive interest without declaration of tax from UK bank and building society accounts. Strictly speaking such interest is not tax-free and would be taken into account by HMRC when considering how any claim to use personal allowances was applied. For this and other tax-related reasons, the normal advice is that the expatriate should open an offshore bank account – typically in the Channel Islands or Isle of Man – and close UK-based deposits. Interest from offshore accounts is paid gross and will be free of UK tax while the expatriate is non-UK resident.
- New investments ahead of departure should only be made after seeking professional advice. There may be opportunities to structure fresh investments to ensure that profits only arrive once the investor is free of UK tax liabilities.

FINANCIAL PLANNING WHILE OVERSEAS

Provided that the advance preparation has been satisfactory, the best financial planning action that the new expatriate can take in the first few months overseas is to do nothing. The reason for this is that it will take the new expatriate at least this period to adjust to the new life and pattern of expenditure. Once settled into a routine, the expatriate will be much more aware of what he or she can save on a regular basis.

Existing investments

A change introduced by the 1998 Budget significantly reduced the capital gains tax advantages of being an expatriate. As a general rule, for the expatriate who has been resident and UK ordinarily resident for at least four out of the seven tax years before departure overseas and who will be non-UK resident and not UK ordinarily resident for less than five tax years, any capital gains realised on investments held before leaving the UK will remain subject to UK capital gains tax. For these 'short-term' expatriates, the 1998 change limits the scope for realising large gains, as might, for example, have accrued from the exercise of share options. Even for the expatriate who expects to be abroad for five or more tax years, caution is necessary until the five-year point is reached; a premature return to the UK could occur for any number of reasons, including health, business or even war. Be aware also of changes in the indexation rules relating to capital gains that are foreshadowed for the 2008 Finance Act.

Income from UK shares and unit trusts will usually continue to be subject to UK tax, which will generally not be reclaimable. There may also be a liability in the host country, although this will often be reduced or eliminated as a result of double taxation agreements.

New investments

Aside from monies placed in Channel Island/Isle of Man deposit accounts (see above), professional advice should always be sought before making investments while overseas. Ideally the advice should be from a firm regulated in the UK by the Financial Services Authority (FSA). Any advice should take into account potential host-country tax liabilities – a point sometimes overlooked by UK-based advisers.

The obvious first port of call for new investments is the offshore financial centres, including Luxembourg, Bermuda and Dublin, as well as the islands closer to home. While certain offshore investments can offer tax benefits to expatriates, these may be offset by higher charges than apply in the UK. Investments made while overseas will usually escape UK capital gains tax provided that gains are realised before the tax year of return to the UK.

Consideration must always be given to what happens to the investment on return to the UK because the tax-efficient investment for the non-UK resident can turn into a tax-inefficient investment for the UK resident. This can be a particular problem if an overseas employment is terminated at short notice.

Expatriates should avoid committing themselves to fixed-term savings contracts as a way of accumulating funds while non-resident. Lack of flexibility can be a serious drawback in many of these schemes, although they are heavily promoted.

Wherever you have a family get together

AXA PPP healthcare is right there with you

For great British healthcare – worldwide – join us now and we'll give you two months' cover free

Call +44(0)1892 550817 quoting reference WA2006 or visit www.axapphealthcare.co.uk/wa

PPP HEALTHCARE

Be Life Confident

PPP HEALTHCARE

When you are considering buying any insurance policy it is always important to bear in mind what you are covered for and if you have specific requirements or considerations.

Alongside its International Health Plan, AXA PPP healthcare has relationships with partner companies in Europe and the Middle East.

If you are thinking of, or currently live or work in, Malta, Cyprus, Bahrain, UAE, Saudi Arabia or Egypt you can benefit from unique, tailor-made, health plans which have been established with our partners in these countries to meet local healthcare needs.

Atlas Insurance agency is Malta's largest agency operation and its roots go back 100 years as one of the first agencies in Malta for a major British insurance company. The company is a product of a merger between 3 major British general insurance agencies and more recently AXA Insurance. Atlas has now created a specialist agency for healthcare, Atlas Healthcare Insurance Agency Limited and has been selling a range of PMI products for AXA PPP healthcare since its appointment in May 2000.

Atlas Insurance Agency Ltd
Ms Claudine Gauci
Health Insurance Department
Abate Rigord Street
Ta'Xbiex
MSD 12
Malta
Telephone: (356) 21 322600

Universal Life has been in partnership with AXA PPP healthcare since 1995 having been established in 1970. It acts as AXA PPP healthcare's partner in Cyprus. It is one of the largest medical insurers on the island having entered the market in 1987.

Universal Life
Mr Stelios Sofroniou
Universal Tower
85 Dhigenis Akritas Avenue
PO Box 21270, 1505 Nicosia
Cyprus
Telephone: 00 357 22 882222

AXA Insurance and AXA PPP healthcare formed a partnership in the United Arab Emirates in July 2002. Both companies are part of the same leading global group, AXA. With operations in more than 60 countries, the strength of AXA, with AXA PPP healthcare's 65 years of specialist customer care, offers customers both security and expertise.

AXA Insurance E.C.
The Healthcare Manager
PO Box 32505
Dubai
UAE
Telephone: 00971 4 3436161

Gulf Union's relationship dates back to 1998. Gulf Union operates in Saudi Arabia and Bahrain where it is a leading independent composite insurer since being incorporated in 1982. .

Gulf Union Insurance and Risk Management Co. (EC)
Mr Roy Samuel
PO Box 5719
Dammam 31432
Saudi Arabia
Telephone: 00966 3 8812070

Gulf Union Insurance & Reinsurance
Mr Roy Samuel
PO Box 10949
Manama
Bahrain
Telephone: 00 973 17 257 018 or 00 973 17 255 292

AXA PPP healthcare and Arab Misr Insurance Group (AMIG) have formed a new partnership with AMIG acting as AXA PPP healthcare's partner in Egypt.

AMIG
The Healthcare Manager
29 El Batrawy Street from Abaas El Akaad
Nasr City
Cairo
Egypt
Tel: (0020 2) 262-3557 and 403-3012 Ext. 41, 28 and 19

Share options

The tax treatment of share options held by expatriates is a highly complex subject. For example, under an unapproved scheme, a UK tax liability will arise on exercise by a non-UK-resident employee if the option was granted when the employee was UK resident. Professional advice should be sought before any action is taken, including the initial grant of an option.

THE UK EXPATRIATE – PLANNING FOR RETURN

In an ideal world, every expatriate would spend the year before return to the UK putting his or her financial plans in order. In practice, there may be a last-minute rush, either because the expatriate was too busy with other matters or because the return home was earlier than originally intended.

Pre-return planning is as important as pre-departure planning. The aims should be to minimise the overall tax liabilities on investments before arrival in the UK, and to ensure that any new plans put in place are appropriate upon return to the UK. This will require professional advice, which should begin in the tax year before that in which the return to the UK will take place.

The planning will need to consider UK tax rules alongside host-country tax rules. It may be better to suffer UK tax – at a maximum rate of 40 per cent – rather than host-country tax. In some instances, it could even be worth spending a few days in a third country and realising profits at that interim stage, before becoming UK tax resident but after ceasing to be host-country tax resident.

For 'short-term' expatriates, there will only be scope to avoid UK capital gains tax on investments acquired while overseas, provided that they are not sold in the tax year of return to the UK. The old planning trick of 'bed and breakfast' – selling one day and buying back the next – to realise a gain but to retain the investment is no longer effective. However, the same result can be achieved if one spouse sells and the other buys.

If offshore deposit accounts are used, usually these should be closed immediately before return to the UK so that all interest is crystallised free of UK tax. UK deposit accounts will automatically give rise to taxable interest in the tax year of return, even if interest is paid before the date of physical return.

LETTING AND INSURING YOUR HOME WHILE ABROAD

Most home owners going to live abroad for a limited period will be looking for a tenant to live in their house or flat while they are away. There is, of course, an obvious alternative, which is to sell, but then there is the question of storage of your effects – the average storage charge for the contents of a typical three-bedroomed house will be more than £60 per week – and, more to the point, the fact that when you do return to this country you will have no place of your own to go to. Even if you do not intend to return to the house you lived in when you come back, it may be advisable to retain ownership because your house represents a fairly inflation-indexed asset. Conversely, if you believe that the UK housing market in 2007 was so overheated that the present easing in house prices is likely to persist or even degenerate into a serious decline while you are abroad, there is a strong case for selling up if you are leaving now.

The case for letting, as opposed to leaving your home empty, hardly needs to be put today when crime and vandalism are constantly in the headlines. Long ago, the government, recognising the difficulties for owners leaving their homes and wishing to encourage the private landlord, introduced the 1988 Housing Act which came into force on 15 January 1989. This Act simplified the many provisions of the various Rent and Housing Acts from 1965 to 1988, and introduced the Assured Shorthold Tenancy (AST), making letting safer and easier. The 1988 Act was further amended by the 1996 Housing Act, making an AST the market 'default' type of tenancy agreement as long as certain criteria are met. An AST guarantees possession to a landlord at the end of a tenancy. Lettings to large companies where the occupier is a genuine employee being housed by the company temporarily are excluded from the Act and are simply contractual tenancies (referred to as Company Lets); these types of tenancy are quite common in bigger cities, particularly central London. It is not possible here to define the various differences between these two forms of tenancy. It should be noted that a letting to a member of the Diplomatic Corps based in the UK has some risks and complications. Generally a court order for possession can be executed but successfully imposing any type of monetary court order (for rent arrears or damages) can be very problematical as the individual would be outside the jurisdiction of British courts and may well have returned to his or her country of origin. It is essential, therefore, for the owner to obtain proper advice before deciding which form of tenancy to choose.

Assured shorthold tenancies

1. These can be for any length of time if both parties agree, although it is most common to start with either 6- or 12-month fixed-term tenancies. However, the landlord will not be able to seek a court order for possession before the end of 6 months unless there has been a breach of the tenancy agreement.
2. The rent will be a market rent, although the tenant may apply to the Rent Assessment Committee during the first 6 months if he or she feels it is too high. However, on the expiry of the original term, the owner is entitled to request the tenant to pay a higher rental and the tenant is not entitled to go back to the Rent Assessment Committee. It is common to have rent increase clauses within longer-term tenancy agreements.
3. Two months' notice has to be served that the landlord requires possession on a certain date (but not before the end of the fixed term); if the tenant refuses to leave, the courts must grant possession.

Additional and amended provisions (grounds) for a mandatory possession order have been included in the 1996 Act, such as two months' arrears of rent, and there are a number of discretionary grounds on which possession can be granted, even if the owner does not wish to return to the house. However, there is one specific disadvantage if the owner is unfortunate enough to have a tenant who refuses to leave when the owner wishes to reoccupy and the landlord then has to apply to court. The judicial system in the UK can occasionally take some time to operate and this can be particularly true if a local court happens to be busy. This unfortunately can extend the period needed before a possession order is granted by the court and owners would be well advised to take out one of the various insurance policies now available to cover hotel costs, legal fees, etc, and as a minimum to make sure that either alternative accommodation is temporarily available in the event of an earlier than expected return home, or alternatively ensure that the procedures for terminating the tenancy are instigated well before the projected date of return.

As must now be obvious to the reader, the complexity of the rules does nothing to encourage owners to attempt to let the property or manage their home themselves while away, and the need for an experienced property management firm becomes even more important than in the past. A solicitor might be an alternative but, although possibly more versed in the legal technicalities than a managing agent, he or she will not be in a position to market the house to the best advantage (if at all) and solicitors' practices do not usually have staff experienced in property management, able to carry out inspections, deal with repairs, arrange inventories and to handle the many and various problems that often arise.

Having obtained advice to ensure that you have the correct form of tenancy, you now need to find an experienced and reliable letting and management agent. Ideally, he or she should be a member of the Royal Institution of Chartered Surveyors (RICS), the Association of Residential Letting Agents (ARLA) or the National Association of Estate Agents (NAEA) specialising in property management who will be well versed in both the legal and financial aspects of the property market.

Property management

Property management is a rather specialised role and you should check carefully that the agent you go to can give you the service you need, that he or she is not just an accommodation broker, and that he or she is equipped to handle the letting, collection of rent and management of your property, as well as the more common kinds of agency work. Your solicitor should be able to advise you here, but to some extent you will have to rely on your own judgement of how ready and satisfactory the agent's answers are to the sort of questions you are going to want to ask. There are several specialised firms well equipped to deal with your affairs, but it is best to stick to members of RICS, ARLA and NAEA as they and their activities are all regulated by their professional bodies.

In the first place the agent you instruct should have a clear idea of the kind of tenant you expect for your property, and preferably be able to show you that he or she does have people on his or her books who are looking for rented accommodation of this kind. Obviously the rent and the tenant you can expect will vary with what you have to offer, and an agent who understands the local market well will be able to advise on what additional fixtures and equipment you need to install in order to maximise the rental value. A normal family house in a good area should attract someone like the executive of a multinational company who is in a similar, but reverse, position to your own: that is, someone working here on a contract basis for a limited period of time who may well provide a stable tenancy for the whole or a substantial part of your absence. A smaller house or flat would be more likely to attract a younger person who only wants the property for a limited period or who, at any rate, might be reluctant to accept a long-term commitment because of the possibility of a change in professional circumstances or marital status. Equally, if you are only going to be away for a shortish period like 6 to 12 months, you are going to be rather lucky to find a tenant whose needs exactly overlap with your absence. You will probably have to accept a slightly shorter period than your exact stay abroad.

For your part you should bear in mind that tenants, unlike house purchasers, are usually only interested in a property with almost immediate possession, but you should give the agent, wherever possible, at least four to six weeks' warning of your departure in order that interest may be built up by advertising, mailing out details, etc, over a period of time.

Rent

How much rent you can expect will also vary with what you have to offer and where it is, but the point to bear in mind is that rents are not usually subject to bargaining like the price of a house. Bargaining, if there is to be any, is more likely to occur over the terms of the lease, which are set out below. Do not, therefore, ask for an unrealistically high figure in the expectation that the tenant will regard this as a starting point for negotiation. Your agent, if he or she knows the job, will be able to advise you on the rental you should ask, though if you have not had previous dealings with him or her it might be advisable to ask the agent to give you some instances of rentals being achieved in the market for similar accommodation. An offer that is a bit less than you had hoped for, but from a good tenant, might be worth taking in preference to a better one from somebody who, for various reasons, looks more doubtful.

Terms of agreement

A property management agent should have, or be able to produce fairly quickly, a draft agreement to cover the specific situation of the overseas landlord. Member agents of the three professional bodies all have access to model agreements that take account of the various pieces of legislation and will have been drafted taking account of the Unfair Terms in Consumer Contract Regulations which impact heavily on what can and cannot be said in such agreements. You should show this to your solicitor, and how well it is drafted will again be a pointer to how effective the agent concerned is likely to be. The document should cover at least the following points:

1. The intervals of payment – monthly or quarterly – and the length of lease.
2. How much the tenancy deposit is to be and where it will be held, and the process for dealing with damages disputes at the end of the tenancy. (NB: from October 2006 the government is introducing legislation to protect tenancy deposits and any AST will have to include by law certain clauses about this.)
3. An undertaking by the tenant to take steps to reasonably maintain the garden.
4. An undertaking by the tenant to pay for telephone and other services from the commencement of the lease, including Council Tax.
5. An undertaking to allow the landlord, or the agent, access to the property (upon lawful notice) for inspection and repair; and two months before the expiry of the lease to allow him or her to take other prospective tenants or purchasers round the property.
6. A clause stating that the lease is terminated if any of the other clauses are broken, although the wording has to be carefully drafted to avoid invalidating the agreement.
7. What you, as landlord, are responsible for in the way of repairs: usually the maintenance of the structure and furnishings of the property together with anything left in the property (eg the central heating boiler). You can exclude some items, such as the television, from your responsibility, but generally the tenant is only liable for specific damage to items left in the house and not for their general maintenance. The

government has tightened up safety laws in respect of gas appliances. In November 1994 the Gas Safety (Installation & Use) Regulations 1994 were introduced, forcing landlords to take greater responsibility for the safety of their tenants by regularly servicing and repairing any gas appliances through a British Gas or Corgi registered company. A landlord has to provide a tenant annually with a Gas Safety Record. Heavy penalties will be enforced for failing to comply.

8. Any special restrictions you want to impose: if, for example, your house is full of valuable antiques you may wish to specify 'no small children'.

9. Notice under Sections 47 and 48 of the Landlord and Tenant Act 1987. The former should be on all rent demands; the latter, notifying the tenant of an address in England or Wales at which notices can be served on the landlord, need only be served once on a tenant at the beginning of a tenancy.

Although the agreement is probably the central document in the transactions involved in letting your house, it does not bring to an end all the things you have to think about. For instance, there is the important matter of the contents insurance. Letting your home to a third party is probably not covered in your policy and you will have to notify your insurers (and the people who hold your mortgage) that this is what you are doing. In many instances, insurance companies will not insure the contents if the property is to be let and you will need to check carefully that you have cover and switch to another company if it becomes necessary. (This is covered in greater detail on pages 82–84, under Insurance.) At the same time you would be wise to check that the contents insurance covers the full value of what you have left in the house. This check could be combined with making a proper inventory of the contents, which is in any case essential before tenants move into a furnished property. Making an exact inventory is quite a time-consuming business and you should bear in mind that it will also have to be checked at the end of the lease, when you may not be there. There are several firms that provide a specialist inventory service at both ends of the lease, covering dilapidations as well as items actually missing, for quite a modest charge which, incidentally, is deductible from the tax due from the letting. Any good management agent should be able to put you on to one of them or will provide an in-house inventory service.

It is also essential that landlords are aware of important fire regulations that have come into force concerning the supply of furniture and furnishings when letting out accommodation. The Furniture (Fire) (Safety) Regulations 1988, introduced for all landlords on 1 January 1997, make it an offence to supply furniture which does not comply with the regulations concerning fire resistance. Essentially, it covers all upholstery and upholstered furnishings, including loose fittings and permanent or loose covers. These must comply with the following three tests, each of which measures the flame-retardant properties of the furnishings: Cigarette Test; Match Test; Ignitability Test. Heavy penalties will be enforced for failing to comply. Your managing agent should be able to provide details of exactly what furniture should be removed or replaced and when.

Finding the tenant and getting a signature on the agreement marks the beginning rather than the end of the property management firm's responsibilities. Broadly, these fall under two headings: the collection of rental and the management of the property. The rent is collected from the tenant, usually on a standing order basis, under the terms – monthly or quarterly – as set out in the agreement; and, in the event of persistent non-payment, the agent will instruct solicitors on your behalf to issue a County Court summons, or if you have taken out rental or legal insurance, the agent will contact the insurance company.

What can you expect from the agent?

The letting and residential managing agent should be regulated. Most commonly this means being a member of the Association of Residential Letting Agents, ARLA. This is the only professional body that is solely concerned with letting and renting and the management of residential property. To be a member of ARLA, the agent must be fully compliant with client accounts, professional indemnity insurance and the ARLA bonding scheme. Every ARLA member office must employ staff with relevant qualifications. Should it be felt that the agent has not performed satisfactorily, ARLA operates an independent redress system.

To check whether or not an agent is an ARLA member, or to find one, or for advice on letting your property or buying to let, visit www.arla.co.uk.

Management is a more complex subject, but an experienced property management agent should be able to supply you with a list of the services that he or she can undertake. It is, therefore, also a checklist of the kind of eventualities that may crop up in your absence which, broadly speaking, relate to the collection of rent, the payment of charges such as service charges and insurance, arrangements for repairs to the fabric of the building and its contents, garden maintenance, and forwarding mail.

Thus, apart from the basic business of collecting the rent, the agent can also pay, on your behalf, any charges on the property (eg, ground rent, water rates and insurance) that your contract with the tenant does not specify should be paid by him or her. There may also be annual maintenance agreements to pay in respect of items like central heating plant and the washing machine.

Then there is the question of what to do about repairs. As we have indicated earlier, whatever you manage to get the tenant to agree to take care of under the terms of the lease, there are certain responsibilities for maintenance and repair that you have to accept by virtue of your status as a landlord. If repairs are necessary, you will simply have to trust the agent to obtain fair prices for you.

On the other hand, except in the case of essential repairs that affect the tenant's legal rights of enjoyment of the property, you can ask your agent to provide estimates for having the work carried out, so that your approval must be obtained before the job is put in hand. Bear in mind, though, that in certain parts of the world the postal system may not be all that reliable. You may, therefore, find it a good idea to put a clause in the management contract giving the agent freedom to proceed with the best estimate if he or she does not hear from you within a specified period. For the same reason it is also wise to ask the agent to send you a formal acknowledgement of receipt of any special or new instructions you have given. An example of this might be an instruction to inspect the property at regular intervals.

To summarise, the responsibilities of a property management agent are as follows:

- collection of rent;
- day-to-day tenant liaison;
- general supervision of the property;
- payment of service charges and insurance;
- arranging repairs to the building and contents;
- payment of charges on the property;

- payment of maintenance agreements;
- obtaining prices/estimates for repairs.

Depending on how many concessions you have to make to the tenant to get him or her to sign the lease, there may be other articles for which repair and maintenance remain your responsibility. These may include the washing machine, TV and the deep freeze. Such responsibilities should be set out in the management contract and you should give the agent the details of any guarantees or maintenance contracts relating to them and photocopies of the actual documents for reference. If no such arrangements apply, you should list the manufacturers' names and the model number and age of each item so that the agent can get the manufacturer to send the repair people along equipped with the right spares.

It is very important that a third party, other than you and the tenant, should be in possession of all this information, particularly when there is likely to be more than one tenancy during your absence; and it is a competent management agent, rather than friends, relatives or even a solicitor, who will be best equipped in this case to find new tenants, to check their references, to draw up new agreements and supervise the handover of the tenancy.

Costs and tax

The costs of all these services vary according to the nature of the package you need. For example, the charge for letting and collection is usually 10 per cent of annual rental. In the case of management services, expect to find additional charges made (usually 5 to 7 per cent of the annual rent). These are reasonable fees for the quite considerable headaches involved. We have shown enough of them here to indicate that not only is it virtually impossible to administer a tenancy yourself from a distance, but also that these are not matters to be left to an amateur – friend or relative – however well intentioned. In real terms the agent's charges may be reduced because they are deductible against the tax levied in the UK against rental income.

Expatriates letting their homes also derive a further benefit in respect of capital gains tax. Generally, if you let your principal residence, when you come to sell it you can claim exemption from CGT only for those years in which you lived in it yourself. However, if you let it because you are absent abroad this does not apply, provided you come back to live in the house before you sell it.

Finally, in this context, it is worth pointing out that some mortgage lenders are now prepared to consider giving mortgages to expatriates for the purchase of a property in the UK *and* to allow them to lease that property for the period of their stay overseas. Up to 90 per cent of the purchase price is available at normal rates of interest. This is an attractive proposition for expatriates, particularly for young executives and professional people who have not yet bought a home in the UK but are earning a substantial income in, say, the Middle East, and for older expatriates perhaps thinking of a retirement home in the UK.

Some agencies supply details of the lenders offering this facility, or you could approach a lender directly and explain your position. Should you buy a house as an expatriate and then let it until you return, the earlier recommendation that you leave the management of the property to an experienced and competent agent still applies. If a UK property is bought purely as an investment, you would have to time its sale carefully to avoid liability for CGT.

Taxation is too complex a subject and varies considerably in its effects on the individual, preventing any practical advice being offered other than to state the importance of employing the services of an accountant in your absence, but it must be stressed that rent received in the UK is considered unearned income, and is subject to UK tax laws. A new scheme now operates whereby letting agents, or where there are no letting agents, tenants of a non-resident landlord, must deduct tax at the basic rate from the rental income, and pay tax quarterly to Her Majesty's Revenue and Customs. Those landlords who wish to receive their income with no tax deducted can apply to CNRL for approval. Forms are available from: CNRL (non-residents), St John's House, Merton Road, Bootle, Merseyside L69 9BB; tel: 0151 472 6208/6209.

Insurance

One important point that is often overlooked by people who let their house or flat is the necessity of notifying the insurers that a change of occupancy has taken place. Insurance policies only cover occupancy by the insured, not the tenants, though they can be extended to do so on payment of what is usually only a small premium. As many insurance companies will not cover properties that are or will be let, notifying the company concerned becomes essential.

What worries insurance companies much more is if the house is left unoccupied for any length of time. If you look at your policy you will see that it lapses if you leave your house empty for more than 30 days or so – a point that is sometimes forgotten by people who go away on extended holidays. If you are going abroad and leave the house empty – maybe because you have not yet succeeded in finding a tenant – the insurers will usually insist that you turn off the main services and that the premises are inspected regularly by a qualified person. That means someone like a letting agent, not a relative or friend. Even if you have let the house without an agent, it may still be advisable to get one to look after the place. A situation could easily occur where the tenant moves out, leaving the place empty and without satisfactory steps having been taken from an insurance point of view. Furthermore, if the worst happens and the house is broken into or damaged, it is imperative that the insurers are notified right away. The effects of damage can be made worse if they are not rapidly attended to, and insurers do not hold themselves responsible for anything that happens between the time the insured eventuality occurs and the time they are notified of it. For instance, if your house is broken into and, a few days later, vandals get in through a broken point of entry and cause further damage, you would not be covered for that second incident unless the insurers had been notified of the first break-in.

Valuable contents are best put into storage and insured there. Pickfords, for instance, charges a premium of 12.5 per cent of the storage charge, inclusive of insurance premium tax (IPT). For contents worth more than £25,000, a reduction may be possible. For very high-value items, safe deposit boxes are becoming popular, but from an everyday point of view, the important thing is to make sure you are insured for full values. If you insure contents for £15,000 and the insurer's assessors value them at £20,000 you will only get three-quarters of your claim. To keep insured values in line with rising costs, an index-linked policy would be the best buy for anyone contemplating a long stay abroad. A policy specially written for expatriates is available from Europea-IMG Ltd: the Weavers Homeowners Policy. It also offers expatriate motor insurance on private cars being used overseas. All insurance premiums are now subject to IPT.

Insuring at full value, incidentally, is equally important when it comes to insuring contents and personal belongings in your residence abroad. Many items will cost much more locally if you have to replace them than they did at the time they were originally bought. There are a few such policies available in the UK, or it may be possible to insure in the country concerned.

Finally, but most importantly, you should insure against legal and hotel costs when letting your house. Although in principle the legal instruments for quick repossession exist, events have shown that a bloody-minded tenant with a committed lawyer can spin things out to his or her advantage for almost an indefinite period. Premiums, which can be offset against rental income, are in the region of £85 a year.

Also recently introduced are rental protection policies, some providing limited cover at a relatively low premium, others covering the higher rental amounts, which are naturally more expensive. In addition, these policies will normally cover legal and other costs. However, due to the wide cover involved, the insurance companies usually insist on their own credit check and the employment of a managing agent, as well as the usual references.

The same companies will add, as an extra, buildings and/or contents cover when the property is let, often at rates that are competitive to the premiums charged when the property was owner-occupied.

Checklist: Financial planning and the expatriate

1. Check out your financial adviser's credentials.
2. Consider the pros and cons of offshore funds.
3. Check your life assurance policy to make sure that there are no restrictions about overseas living.
4. Consider tax-efficient ways to save for school fees.
5. If your company has a pension scheme in the country of residence, make sure you become acquainted with its rules and local legislation through your financial adviser.
6. Notify your financial adviser at least 12 months before the tax year of your return so that he or she can mitigate tax liabilities.

Checklist: Letting your home

1. Take professional advice about the most appropriate type of tenancy and the likely rental level, terms, etc.
2. Remember to take account of notice periods when planning your return.
3. Ask your property management agent to explain to you what kinds of people he or she has on the books.
4. Try to give the agent six to eight weeks warning prior to the rental date.
5. Seek advice from your solicitor concerning the agent's draft contract.
6. Inform your insurance company (and your mortage lender) of your intention to let your home and check that your contents insurance covers the full value of what you have left in the house.
7. Make a full inventory of the contents.
8. Ensure that your furniture complies with fire regulations.
9. Provide your agent with details of any guarantees or maintenance contracts.
10. Put valuable possessions into storage.
11. Consider insuring against legal and hotel costs.

The sections in this chapter on offshore banking are provided by Lloyds TSB Bank plc, and on foreign exchange by No1currency. The editor expresses his thanks for use of the material.

6 National Insurance, Benefits and Pensions

The desire to earn more money – and to pay less of it in tax and other deductions – looms large for many as a motive for going to work abroad. People who take this step are often temperamentally inclined to be strongly individualistic and self-reliant and, as such, many feel that they would rather fend for themselves when circumstances get difficult rather than rely on what they regard as 'state handouts'. Whatever the virtues of this attitude of mind may be, those who have it are more to be commended for their sense of independence than their common sense. The fact is that during your working life in the UK you will have made compulsory National Insurance contributions and you are therefore eligible for benefits in the same way as if you had paid premiums into a private insurance scheme; drawing a state benefit you are entitled to is no more taking a handout than making an insurance claim.

National Insurance has another feature in common with private insurance: you lose your entitlement to benefit if you fail to keep up your contributions, though the circumstances under which this would happen are different from, and more gradual than in, the private sector. Furthermore, you cannot immediately reactivate your eligibility for benefits in full if, your payments having lapsed for a period of time, you return to this country and once again become liable to make contributions. For instance, in order to qualify in full for a UK retirement pension you must have paid the minimum contribution for each year for at least 90 per cent of your working life. In the case of other benefits too, in order to qualify to get them, there must be a record of your having made a certain level of contributions in the two tax years governing that in which benefits are being claimed.

DWP AGENCIES

National Insurance provisions are handled by Executive Agencies of the Department for Work and Pensions (DWP) (website: www.dwp.gov.uk). The Contributions Agency deals with all contributions and insurability matters, while the Benefits Agency deals with all matters relating to social security benefits.

NI contribution matters for persons working abroad are handled by the Contributions Agency's International Services, Longbenton, Newcastle upon Tyne NE98 1YX; tel: 0845 915 4811. The International service can provide you with information on your National Insurance liability, voluntary contributions, retirement pension forecasts, health care and other benefits. Visit the website at www.inlandrevenue.gov.uk/nic/intserv/osc.htm. Matters relating to benefits are handled by the Benefit Agency's Pensions and Overseas Benefits Directorate at Tyneview Park, Newcastle upon Tyne NE98 1BA; tel: 0191 218 7777.

Leaflet NI 38, or for European Economic Area countries leaflet SA29, available from either Agency at Newcastle, or from a local social security office, sets out the basic conditions relating to National Insurance and benefits abroad.

LIABILITY FOR CONTRIBUTIONS WHILE ABROAD

If your employer in the UK sends you to work in another European Economic Area country or in a country with which the UK has a reciprocal agreement (these are listed in leaflet NI 38) for a period not expected to exceed that which is specified in the EC regulations *or* the reciprocal agreement (RA) involved, you will normally continue to be subject to the UK social security scheme for that period and you will be required to pay Class 1 contributions as though you were in the UK. (The specified period can vary between one year where the EC regulations apply and up to five years depending upon the reciprocal agreement involved.) If your employment unexpectedly lasts longer than 'the specified period', then for certain countries you may remain insured under the UK scheme with the agreement of the authorities in the country in which you are working. Your employer will obtain a certificate for you from the Contributions Agency, International Services, at Newcastle upon Tyne confirming your continued liability under the UK scheme, which you should present to the foreign authorities if required to confirm your non-liability under their scheme. This form, E101, is issued with European Health Cards which provide health care cover abroad for you and your family for the period of employment in another country.

If you are sent by your UK employer to an EU member state or to a country with which there is a reciprocal agreement in circumstances other than the above, eg for an initial period expected to exceed 12 months or for a period of indefinite duration, then normally you will cease to be liable to pay UK contributions from the date you are posted and will instead become liable to pay into the scheme of the country you are working in. Leaflet SA29 tells you about the European Community (EC) Regulations on social security and their effect on EU nationals. If you would like a copy of leaflet SA29 or would like more information, you can telephone or write to International Services. Alternatively you can get a copy of leaflet SA29 from your local social security office.

If you are sent by your employer to a country other than those in the EU or with which there is a reciprocal agreement, you will be liable to pay Class 1 contributions for the first 52 weeks of your posting provided your employer has a place of business in the UK, you were resident in the UK immediately before you took up employment abroad, you remain 'ordinarily resident' in the UK while you are abroad and you are under UK retirement age (currently 60 for women and 65 for men). If you are self-employed you must obtain forms E101/E102/E128.

MAKING VOLUNTARY CONTRIBUTIONS

For non-EU and non-RA countries, when your period of liability for Class 1 contributions ends, you may wish to pay voluntary Class 3 contributions to the UK scheme in order to protect your UK retirement/widow's pension entitlement. We will deal with the mechanics of this later, but at this stage it should be pointed out that if you are going abroad for a British-based firm you will be liable to make the same contributions as if you were employed in this country up to a maximum earnings level of £770 per week (2008/2009 tax year). Your proportion of this contribution will be deducted from your salary, as if you were still working in the UK. Payment of these contributions for the first 52 weeks of your employment abroad will make you eligible to receive incapacity or unemployment benefit and, in the case of a woman, maternity allowance, under the usual conditions applicable to those benefits, on your return to the UK – even though this may be some years later – because Class 1 contributions will be deemed to have been paid in the tax year(s) relevant to your claim. This is subject to the proviso that you remained 'ordinarily resident' in the UK during your absence. If you did not intend to sever your connection with the UK when you went abroad, continuing ordinary residence will usually be accepted. To establish ordinary residence you may need to show that you maintained a home or accommodation in the UK or stored your furniture in the UK during your absence. To maintain entitlement to UK retirement pension or widow's benefits, however, it will usually be necessary to pay Class 3 contributions after the Class 1 period has expired although this may not be necessary for the balance of the year – April to April – in which Class 1 liability ceased. The Contributions Agency, International Services, Room BP1303, Longbenton, Newcastle upon Tyne NE98 1ZZ can advise you about this. Remember always to quote your National Insurance number and the country involved when you write.

Class 1 contributions are not payable at all in respect of employment abroad if your employer has no place of business in the UK. However, if you work for an overseas government or an international agency such as the UN, you will be able to pay your share of the Class 1 contribution for the first 52 weeks of your employment abroad and so qualify on return to the UK for the benefits named in the previous paragraph.

You may, of course, have been a self-employed person paying the Class 2 rate of £2.30 a week for the 2008/09 tax year. These contributions also cover a more limited range of benefits – Jobseeker's Allowance (previously unemployment benefit) and injury or death caused by an industrial accident or prescribed disease are excluded – but like Class 3 contributions, they can also be paid voluntarily if you go to work in an EU country or countries with which the UK has an RA agreement, provided you are gainfully occupied there. However, you *need not* pay Class 2 contributions just because you were self-employed before you went abroad. You can go to the voluntary Class 3 rate (which is £8.10 for the 2008/2009 tax year), but if you want to qualify for incapacity benefit when you return to the UK, provided you were employed abroad you can switch back to Class 2 payments for the two tax years governing the benefit year in which you are due to return. Advice for those who are self-employed is available from the National Insurance Contributions Office, Self-Employment Services, Benton Park View, Newcastle upon Tyne NE98 1ZZ, or by ringing the Helpline (0845 915 4515) and quoting your National Insurance number.

These rates and conditions apply, of course, as much to women as to men. The right of married women to pay reduced rate contributions has been phased out. If you get married while working abroad you should write to International Services for leaflet CA13 which explains in more detail your National Insurance position as a married woman. A married woman may consider paying contributions in her own right (eg for retirement pension purposes). See leaflet NI 38.

Leaflet NI 38 contains a form at the back (CF83) which should be filled in when you want to start making voluntary payments. You can pay by annual lump sum, by arranging for someone in the UK to make regular payments for you, or through direct debit if you have a bank or building society in the UK or Channel Islands.

Class 2 and Class 3 contributions can be paid before the end of the sixth tax year following the one in which they were due. However, although you have six years in which to pay there is a limited period in which to pay at the relevant year's contribution rates. International Services can advise you about this. Whatever method you choose it is important that your contributions are paid on time. For further information see leaflet CA07 – *Unpaid and late paid contributions*. Also see CF411 *How to protect your State Retirement Pension*.

GETTING NI BENEFITS ABROAD

Thus far we have only mentioned the range of benefits available to you once you return to the UK. But is there any way you can become eligible for benefits while still abroad? Generally, the answer is that you can only receive retirement pensions and widow's benefits, but there are important exceptions in the case of EU countries and some others – a full list is given in leaflet NI 38 – with which the UK has reciprocal agreements. How those agreements affect you varies somewhat from country to country, but in essence they mean that the contributions you have paid in the UK count, for benefit purposes, as if you had paid them in the reciprocal agreement country, and vice versa. This is usually advantageous if you do become eligible for benefit while abroad because in relation to the cost of living – or even in absolute terms – UK benefits are lower than many foreign ones. You will, in general, have to pay contributions to the scheme of the country you are working in, so by the same token if you are going to a country with which the UK has a reciprocal agreement, you will have to decide if you want to pay voluntary contributions to the UK in order to maintain UK pension entitlement when you return here. The Contributions Agency can advise you on this. If you have not yet come under the scheme of a foreign country and are paying Class 1, 2 or 3 contributions to the UK while working abroad then, if you think you are eligible for benefit, you should write to the Benefits Agency, Pensions and Overseas Benefits Directorate immediately the contingency governing your claim arises. One important point to bear in mind in this case, though, is that if benefit can be paid, you will only get paid at the UK rate, not that of similar welfare schemes of the country in which you are living. In many cases the latter may be much more generous than UK rates; furthermore, UK rates may bear very little relationship to the cost of living abroad.

In this connection it is also worth pointing out that the UK is by no means the top of the world league table when it comes to the percentage of the pay packet taken up by contributions to social services. In many of the EU countries, in particular, it is significantly higher. This is an important detail to discuss with a prospective employer, because the 'social wage' and what you have to put in to get it obviously have a bearing on the real value of the remuneration package you are being offered.

THE NHS AND HEALTH CARE BENEFITS

In one important instance UK benefits are actually more generous than those of many other countries. We refer here to the UK National Health Service. But medical expenses incurred abroad are definitely not refunded by the NHS, which is only available to people living in this country; so, contrary to popular belief, you will no longer be able to get free NHS treatment in this country once you become permanently resident abroad. Many overseas countries do have reciprocal health agreements with the UK – once again a list is given on the HMRC site – but the services they provide are not exactly comparable with those of the British NHS. European Health Cards are available from the DSS or post offices and are essential documents in being able to access this reciprocal care. See also leaflet T5 – *Health Advice for Travellers Anywhere in the World*. The range of treatment provided free of charge varies considerably and it is advisable to take out private health insurance to cover eventualities where free medical attention is not, or is only partially, available. Leaflets giving information on the procedures you need to observe, both in the case of temporary spells and permanent residence abroad, are available from the Contributions Agency's International Services (tel: 0845 915 4811 or 44-191-225 4811 if calling from abroad).

CHILD BENEFITS WHILE WORKING ABROAD

There are various situations which, in different ways, affect your entitlement to receive child benefit while working abroad:

1. If you go abroad permanently, taking your children with you, your child benefits cease from the date of your departure. When you arrive in the new country you can only rely on that country's family benefit.
2. If you go to work in another EU country you will generally be insured under its social security legislation and so entitled to the local family allowances. If you are insured under another EU scheme but leave your children behind in Great Britain, you may still be entitled to family allowances from the EU country in which you are insured. If you remain insured under the Great Britain scheme, child benefit may still be payable whether your children are in Great Britain or with you. If your children are not with you, you would have to maintain them by at least the weekly rate of child benefit after the first 56

days. If your children live with you but your spouse or partner is insured under another EU scheme, you will be entitled to local family allowances. However, you may be paid a 'supplement' equal to the difference between the local rate and the Great Britain rate of benefit if the Great Britain rate is higher.

3. If you have been sent abroad to work temporarily, for a period of not more than eight weeks, and you return within that time, benefit will continue to be paid whether or not you take your children with you. Child benefit orders cannot be cashed outside Great Britain, but you will be able to cash them when you return, provided each order is cashed within three months of the date stamped on it. After eight weeks of temporary absence, your eligibility for Great Britain child benefit ceases unless you happen to be in one of the reciprocal agreement countries.

4. You can also continue to be eligible for Great Britain child benefit, even after eight weeks of absence, if in the relevant tax year at least half your earnings from the employment which took you abroad are liable to United Kingdom income tax. However, in this case your entitlement cannot be decided until your tax liability has been assessed.

5. If a child is born abroad within eight weeks of the mother's departure from Great Britain and she is abroad only temporarily, child benefit may be paid from then until the end of the eight-week period of absence. If you wish to claim in these circumstances you should write to the Child Benefit Centre (Washington), PO Box 1, Newcastle upon Tyne NE88 1AA, quoting your child benefit number if you are already getting child benefit for another child.

6. Special rules exist in respect of serving members of the forces and civil servants; persons falling into these categories should consult their paying officer or Establishments Division.

Full details of these schemes, including the form CH 181(TO) which you have to fill in before your departure, are set out in leaflet CH 6, available from your local Social Security office. Alternatively, you can get a copy by writing to the Information Division, Leaflet Unit, Block 4, Government Buildings, Honeypot Lane, Stanmore, Middlesex HA7 1AY.

UNEMPLOYMENT BENEFITS FOR JOB HUNTERS WITHIN THE EU

Under EU law you can go jobseeking for up to three months in most EU countries, provided you have been registered as unemployed in the UK for four weeks before departure. You are entitled to receive Jobseeker's Allowance on the day of departure and you actually register for work in the new country. While you are in the other country, you can continue drawing UK Jobseeker's Allowance via the employment services of the country you are in provided you follow their control procedures.

You should inform your local unemployment benefit office *in person* of your intention well in advance of your departure, and obtain from them leaflet UBL 22. The Pensions and Overseas Benefits Directorate of the Benefits Agency will then issue the authorisation form E303 to you if you are going to France, Greece, Portugal, Spain, Germany or Italy and there is enough time before your departure. Otherwise, it will be sent to your address there. If you are going to another EU country, the form will be sent to a liaison office in the country concerned. Regardless of which country you are going to, ask your local unemployment benefits office to issue you with a letter of introduction. You should give this – and form E303 if you have it – to the employment services when registering for work in another EU country.

In practice, many EU countries have blocked this progressive move by putting obstacles in the way over such matters as residence permits – France is particularly bad in this respect – because the UK is not alone among European Union countries in having an unemployment problem. The good news is that if you do succeed in getting a job in an EU country, in some states not only are wages and salaries higher but so also are unemployment benefits. If you are unlucky enough to lose your 'new' job after being insurably employed under the social security scheme of an EU country, your previous UK insurance may be taken into account to help you become eligible for unemployment benefits which are very much higher than those in the UK.

All Jobcentres now handle vacancies in the EU and can give further details on relevant legislation and social welfare provisions. The Employment Service issues a useful leaflet on these matters, called *Working Abroad*, as well as others detailing conditions in individual countries.

UK PENSION SCHEMES AND THE EXPATRIATE

UK pension schemes have been affected by changes in the state provisions introduced since July 1988. Many pension experts think that employees of companies contracted in to the state scheme, known as SERPS, might be better advised to set up a personal pension scheme which the new legislation now allows them to do, on an individual basis. The value of such a step would depend on a wide variety of circumstances, such as age, whether the expatriate has taxable income in the UK, and if the employer has a contracted out pension scheme, just how good the benefits of its scheme are. Under the Welfare Reform and Pensions Act 1999, UK employers who do not provide either a final salary scheme with defined benefits or a money purchase pension under a defined contributions scheme are obliged to offer access to a stakeholder pension scheme. The issues are very complicated and the taxation rules are subject to change. You should seek advice from a reputable financial management firm with experience of expatriate problems.

Checklist: Working abroad and National Insurance

1. Contact both the Contributions Agency and the Benefit Agency for relevant literature on working abroad and National Insurance contributions.
2. Consider paying voluntary contributions to maintain your benefits entitlement on your return and organise payment through direct debit from your bank or building society while you are away.
3. Check to see if you are still entitled to be paid Child Benefit.
4. If you are looking for work and claiming Jobseeker's Allowance, inform your local unemployment benefits office well in advance of your departure.
5. Take advice on your pension scheme arrangements while working abroad.

Part Three:

Preparing the Family

7 Partner Issues

The success or failure of longer-term foreign assignments nowadays is more often than not affected by the family's willingness to relocate, and the pressures on an expatriate family should not be underestimated. Many families are organised around a dual-income couple with equal weight given to both careers. The problems of accommodating two careers, or for one partner to give up his or hers for the sake of the other, are considerable. Moreover, there is less willingness to send children to boarding school and many employees are accompanied by both partner and offspring to a new location. Creating a fulfilling experience for both partner and children is the key to a successful assignment and this chapter looks at some of the ways in which this may be achieved.

COMPANY ATTITUDES

Enlightened organisations have accepted that the days when the partner was a 'wife', and that a wife did not work, are long gone. Unmarried and dual-earning couples are now frequently the case and, as such, the partner status has become an increasingly urgent problem to sort out. Many partners are unwilling to put their careers on hold. Furthermore, those that do will need help to turn the experience into a worthwhile venture if the employee is to complete the assignment.

It is perhaps no surprise that partners show reluctance to relocate. In a recent survey, relocation company ECA found that, while 65 per cent of expatriates were accompanied by a partner on assignment, of the partners, 60 per cent had worked prior to the assignment but only 16 per cent worked during the assignment. It is quite reasonable to presume that a number of the 44 per cent who didn't work chose not to; however, it is also safe to assume that many would have liked to work, but were not given the opportunity to do so.

With this in mind, larger companies are beginning to recognise the need to provide support to partners. However, these are still a minority, for according to the ECA survey only 12 per cent of companies have established a uniform policy, and of that number, 35 per cent deal with partner careers on a case-by-case basis. Job searches, career counselling, network contacts and educational assistance are some of the ways in which these companies are trying to help partners. Table 7.1 shows the range of company assistance on offer or being considered by organisations.

However, companies with a long-established tradition of expatriation have also begun to develop strategies that see the partner included in the relocation process right from the very start, including the initial selection interview. The inclusion of the partner at this stage not only secures an understanding of his or her needs and expectations but gives a good indication of whether employees have thought through the impact a foreign assignment might have on their personal relationships.

Employees will have the support and structure of the company to help settle in to their new location. The partner, on the other hand, might well be giving up a job, and certainly a social network, to move

Table 7.1   Assistance with partner careers

	Current practice (%)	Considering (%)
Networking contacts	50	10
Work permits	41	11
Education/training assistance	38	22
Career consultancy advice	33	18
Cost of career enhancement	25	12
Access to recruitment specialist	26	17
Arrange employment within company	24	10
Arrange employment with partner's company	6	3
Intra-company database/job swap	2	10

Source: ECA International

to a foreign location without any structure or obvious objective. Recruiters have recognised that it is a false economy not to try to help partners either to find a job or to have a local support network. Failed assignments are costly and many flounder on the trailing partner's desire to return home.

Elisabeth Marx has written about the problems faced by partners in *Breaking Through Culture Shock* and suggests that the pressures are twofold. First, couples experience major problems and crises on international assignments because of the unique situation they find themselves in. Faced with the unpredictability of their situation and having to depend on each other, they are without their social network and normal social controls. Furthermore, Marx points to the fact that in most cases the female partner has to deal with the challenges of settling into a new place. These include organising schooling for the children, sorting out a home and the daily basics, and supporting a partner through the early stages of a new job. Additionally, she will have to try to tap into a social network for the children, and for her and her partner. Add to this the possible demands of her new job, for those who have found one, and one can see why enlightened companies are keen to involve partners from the earliest stage.

Professor Cary Cooper has written extensively about the pressures on dual-income families, and occupational stress. He believes that companies can avoid problems by communicating honestly and inclusively with couples: 'It would seem reasonable that the spouse should be given the "option" to get involved in the decision-making and information-sharing process concerning any move that may impinge on the family. At the moment, organisations are contracting with one element of the family unit, but making decisions which radically affect the unit as a whole. By operating in this way they often cause conflict between the individual and his/her family' (Cooper and Lewis, *The Workplace Revolution*, Kogan Page).

FINDING WORK

The biggest problem for companies is in trying to find career opportunities for the partner in the new location. Apart from being able to find a suitable job to match up to the partner's skills in the new location, there are many parts of the world that will not allow couples to work on one work permit.

If you are a citizen of the European Union original 15 countries (ie live in Austria, Belgium, Denmark, Finland, France, Germany, Greece, Ireland, Italy, Luxembourg, The Netherlands, Portugal, Spain, Sweden or the United Kingdom) and you are being relocated within its borders, there are no such restrictions and partners are allowed to work without a permit.

Outside the European Union, however, work permits for EU citizens are hard to come by, as are permits for non-EU citizens to work in the European Union. In most cases work permits are provided only for the employee who has the backing of an international organisation and a specified job to go to. Dependants are generally allowed resident visas but the opportunity to work on their partner's permit is arbitrary and on the whole limited. For example, Australia allows dependants the right to work on an employee's permit, as does Sweden. Japan, on the other hand, allows part-time work. Islamic countries, such as Saudi Arabia, do not issue work permits to females unless they are in the teaching or nursing professions. Perhaps the most difficult country of all for which to obtain a work permit is the United States, which operates a rigorous immigration policy, unless the partner can show that he or she has unique and rare skills to offer.

Large companies are able to negotiate limited reciprocal arrangements on work permits with other countries, but these tend to be used up by employees. 'In some cases they can go with a joint work permit,' explains John Thompson of PricewaterhouseCoopers, 'in other cases there is a real problem and virtually prohibitive because if you have an unmarried partner, for example, some countries will not give visas. They would not be recognised as a de facto spouse. In some cases we have to say, well, it won't work. As far as we are concerned their status is what it is and if they are going together as an established couple, provided the immigration authorities in the country we are dealing with recognise that, we will do so as well. But we have to look at the practicalities of what can be done.'

Given the difficulties, a few companies will try to find work within their own company for partners with appropriate skills and relocate them in their own right. Others might begin communication with a partner's company to see if there are possibilities for relocation to the same destination within their existing organisation. However, both these, as seen by the ECA survey results, are the least favoured options. Barry Page from Accenture points to further problems, caused by the changing workforce profile, in trying to relocate working partners. 'I have come across organisations where the spouse or partner has a more senior position than the employee and that creates more problems. Also, one cannot presume that the spouse or partner is a female either.'

Many companies find it easier to help partners obtain work permits in their own right rather than to try to do so as a dependant, and to do this have set up network systems and recruitment search facilities to help look for new opportunities. For example, Shell International has set up its OUTPOST website, www.shellspouse employment.com, which provides information to partners who wish to work or develop their skills during and after expatriation. Others provide advice through a career consultancy agency for partners seeking jobs, and advice is given on academic and professional qualifications, and whether training is needed to pursue their career abroad. However, partners looking for work should also think about taking up some of the suggestions in Chapter 1, Independent Job Opportunities, in their search for a job in their own right. Further useful websites are listed at the back of this book.

It is quite possible to look for work once relocated and in situ. However, work permit restrictions might, once again, cause problems and it is worth finding out the situation before leaving for your foreign destination.

FROM EXPAT TO EXPERT

Jonathan Wix, Teacher Recruitment Section, British Council

If you find yourself with time on your hands in a foreign city, your ability to speak English at native fluency is potentially one of your greatest assets. Demand for teachers of English as a Foreign Language (EFL) is high all over the world, and shows no sign of declining. The British Council owns and manages premises equipped for language teaching in almost 50 countries around the world. We offer our students access to great high-tech facilities and resources, but they consistently tell us the best resource we provide is their teacher.

We employ qualified EFL teachers on full-time, part-time and hourly-paid contracts, and from a wide variety of backgrounds. Someone who comes to teaching as a second or third career brings valuable skills and life experience to the work we do. Most of our students are individuals who want English for their work or leisure, but we regularly win contracts from large organisations and businesses that commission us to teach language and other professional skills through English to their staff. There is also high demand for teachers who have the skills to manage a class of school-age children. If you've already taught children or had teacher training, then you have valuable skills for an EFL institute abroad.

Students at the British Council expect to be taught by experts, and we aim to employ the best-qualified candidates. The typical EFL teacher used to be a backpacker or gap-year student, but it's now a credible profession and big business. Without some training, leading to a recognised qualification, your chances of working for a good employer are slim.

The best training courses are those that lead to qualifications that are recognised across the globe. As a guide, we use the Cambridge ESOL Certificate in English Language Teaching to Adults (CELTA) or the Trinity College London Certificate in Teaching English to Speakers of Other Languages (Cert. TESOL), or any course that is their equivalent, as one of our entry-level requirements for all recruits. You can take these courses in many different cities around the world. Go to the relevant websites below for the provider locators. Some British Council centres offer the CELTA course, where your fellow trainees could be local English language teaching specialists from the state system or ex-pat novices.

You don't have to be British to work for the British Council, but you do need to speak English to native ability in order to teach. If you don't have a UK passport, in some countries we would only be able to hire you on a local contract, but the work you do, your status and the rate of pay are the same as for teachers appointed from the UK. Managers will advertise vacancies for local-hire teachers in the local English language press, and maybe on the local British Council website. Since many students have day jobs they come for English lessons after work or at weekends, so the working hours for most teachers are unconventional. If you are looking after family or want to spend time with your partner who's working too, it's important to bear this in mind.

Students are motivated and eager to share their culture as much as learn about others, and through learning English they are learning much more than when to use the present continuous. Our teachers equip their students with skills and attitudes that make them international citizens. With the skills and experience of an EFL teacher you can work pretty much all over the world. If you're not one when you start, it's not long before you become an international citizen yourself.

Websites:

British Council teacher recruitment: http://trs.britishcouncil.org

University of Cambridge ESOL qualifications: www.cambridgeesol.org

Trinity College London ESOL qualifications: www.trinity college.co.uk

Helpful resource for TEFL qualifications: www.cactustefl.com

FURTHER EDUCATION

If finding a job or obtaining a work permit proves too difficult, the time spent abroad might be a chance to explore other avenues. There are several options available to a trailing partner. For example, investigating educational opportunities in a new location could be one avenue for a trailing partner. Universities and business schools might offer an alternative structure and social network to a job. Furthermore, taking a local qualification might aid the process of finding a job in the new location. For example, INSEAD, the French Business School, provides a career service to holders of its MBA.

The internet is also becoming an invaluable educational tool. There is an increasing number of distance learning courses available through the web. As mentioned in Chapter 1, the Open University Business School is one institution that is using electronic means to fully explore educational potential and offers a range of six-month courses on a distance learning basis. Professionals might also use this opportunity to take postgraduate professional qualifications. Professional associations and regulatory bodies will advise you on the availability of distance learning courses. Non-professional education might also be available. For example, learning the language of your host country will provide both practical help and intellectual stimulus.

NETWORKING AND CONSIDERING THE CHILDREN

An invaluable aid to partners is the network of contacts that an employee's company can provide before expatriation. This is not just a way to find out what the location is really like but also provides invaluable contacts on arrival. Shell International has recognised the importance of this and has set up a worldwide information network 'Outpost' of Shell expatriate families, which is run by volunteer Shell partners and spouses. Likewise, PricewaterhouseCoopers encourages contact with expatriates already in location and tries to link up non-working partners.

Once again, the internet has come into its own when considering the opportunities of contacting other expatriate partners. The plethora of websites for expat spouses is too numerous to mention here and is listed in the back of this book. However, apart from the Shell Spouse Centre at www.shellspouseemployment. com, there is also the *Electronic Telegraph*'s expatriate website at www.telegraph.co.uk, Expat Resources for Spouses at www.thesun.org and Expat Forum at www.expatforum.com. Numerous nationality-, location- and occupation-specific forums also exist on the internet and, again, are listed at the back of the book. Furthermore, if your partner's company has not got an expat partner's website, it might also be a good time to enquire as to the possibilities of setting one up.

The focus of settling children in to a new country tends to be placed on schooling, and this will be dealt with in depth in the next chapter. However, it is also important to consider the effect that expatriation will have on their psychological and social development. Each child is, of course, uniquely different and will deal with new situations in his or her own way. For some children the opportunity to experience a new place and meet new people will be regarded as an adventure and will be welcomed. For others, it could be a profoundly disturbing experience, with family and friends disappearing from their daily lives. Older children will also present problems and before relocating it is worth considering how they might find living in a more restrictive or more liberal environment and what kind of freedoms they might expect in comparison to their home culture. Harsh punishments can be handed out for the use of 'soft' drugs and other such misdemeanours in many parts of the world. The example of the flogging of a US teenager for vandalism in Singapore should act as a warning. However, the advice remains consistent. As companies need to include partners in the decision-making process, so too children should be included in preparatory discussions and be given information about their new home. An inclusive process for the whole family might well ease some of the anxiety and stresses of relocation. Likewise, new technology might provide the answer to homesick children who can keep in contact with friends and family through the use of e-mail and the internet. As in other situations, children can act as conductors for the emotional highs and lows of a family and if there is tension and anxiety surrounding the decision to relocate they are also likely to pick this up. Using the time before departure to investigate and research your destination with your children could be a useful exercise for the whole family.

USING YOUR INITIATIVE

No matter how supportive a company might be, in the end the trailing partner role is unlikely to be an easy one. Investigating all the possibilities and opportunities before you go is vital: whether it be job opportunities, further education or building a network of contacts to develop a social life. The last of these might also provide openings that will not become apparent until you have arrived in your new location, such as voluntary work or job opportunities. The stresses and strains on relationships should also be expected and a positive approach to the experience might help ease them. As with your partner's career change, relocation could add to your own career or life expectations by giving you international work experience and/or new skills – such as a language – and by opening new horizons. Having decided to make the move, a flexible approach will be the best way of ensuring that you are open to the opportunities available to you.

Checklist: Partner issues

1. Can you find work in the new location and are your qualifications recognised?
2. Can you work as a dependant or will you have to apply for a work permit in your own right?
3. Is your new location sympathetic to unmarried partners, same-sex partners and women who want to work – all of these can affect your chances of being granted a work permit?

4. Can your company or your partner's company find work within their organisation for you in the new location?

5. What are the educational possibilities in your new location and can your partner's employer help you identify them and/or training opportunities? Consider qualifying as an EFL teacher.

6. Does the company have a network for expat partners either on the internet or through telephone communication?

7. If your company does not have a network for expats, are you in a position to start one yourself?

8. Talk to other expats about the host country's environment for children and give particular thought, if you have teenagers, as to what kind of social life they might be able to have.

9. Involve your children in finding out about the new destination through different media or by making contact with expat children already in situ.

10. Encourage your children to use communications technology to keep in touch with friends and family.

8 Your Children's Education

For those contemplating a job abroad, the issue of schooling cannot be taken lightly. Not only can an unsatisfactory educational solution prejudice a child's chance of achieving academic success, it can also create tensions that have an adverse effect on the home and working environment. In some cases it may lead to the premature termination of overseas contracts.

Educational options certainly demand careful thought and planning. Among the possibilities to be considered are:

1. A boarding school in the UK.
2. A day school in the UK (with guardianships/relatives).
3. An expatriate school abroad.
4. A company-sponsored school abroad.
5. A local national school abroad.
6. Home teaching abroad.

The ultimate choice will be determined by the age, ability and personality of your child, together with the quality of education available abroad and the expected duration of a contract. It will also be based on personal financial considerations and on the education support policy of the employer.

School fees (all, or a substantial part) may be paid by major international companies and organisations, and in some cases by governmental agencies. Whether such an allowance is used to contribute towards education at a UK boarding school or at a local fee-paying school will depend on local availability and the employer's policy. Some of these organisations employ trained staff to offer advice and support. They may also cover travelling expenses to and from the school in the UK, including air fares.

Smaller British companies may indicate that the salary they offer includes an unspecified sum towards the cost of schooling. Locally owned companies, particularly in developing countries, rarely provide an educational allowance.

MAINTAINING CONTINUITY

One factor that must be considered at the outset is that few organisations can be relied upon to give any help with school fees once the assignment abroad has been completed. On return to the UK many parents may find it difficult to finance boarding school fees from a lower, and often more heavily taxed, personal income. However, it can be disruptive to move your children from one school to another and particularly inadvisable at a sensitive stage in their schooling when they have begun a GCSE or A level course. On the other hand, if you have chosen a school abroad with a curriculum that bears little or no resemblance to that followed in the UK, your child may find it hard to cover lost ground. When selecting a school it is crucial to look ahead and to make plans which will serve your child's best interest when your overseas contract comes to an end.

Most schools will go to considerable trouble to make arrangements to see prospective parents, often at short notice. Where possible take your child with you when you visit a school and listen to his or her comments. Whatever your personal feelings about education, it is essential that those of your child are fully respected. Many children have sensible views about what is best for their own development and, where necessary, they should be persuaded rather than instructed.

Your child may be eager to make the transition from state to private school and adapt well to a new environment. However, you should be aware that moving back to the state system can be difficult for ex-independent school pupils. These difficulties can also be encountered by children returning to a local school routine after the cultural diversity of an international educational environment.

The major problem for most children of expatriates is the lack of educational continuity, particularly when they are obliged to move from country to country, and school to school, every few years. If your child is to realise his or her potential you must try to provide educational stability. Much can be done to ease the process of transition by providing a new school with a detailed profile of your child. Reports, syllabus information, titles of books which he or she has been using and levels of attainment can enable a teacher to assist your child to settle happily into life in a new school with the minimum of disruption.

CONTINUED SCHOOLING IN THE UK

Many parents find it difficult to decide whether to send their child to a day or boarding school. For parents who are working overseas boarding is an obvious choice. Indeed, some parents may opt for a job abroad in order to finance their children's education at a boarding school.

How to find a boarding school

Selecting the most appropriate school for your child can be a time-consuming and confusing process, but there are several organisations to help you make your choice.

The Independent Schools Council (ISC), St Vincent House, 30 Orange Street, London WC2H 7HH (tel: 020 7766 7070, website: www.isc.co.uk) produces a number of helpful publications including *Choosing Your Independent School* (£12.95 including postage and packing). They also offer a comprehensive placement service (£350 + VAT), with reductions for siblings, and a consultancy service, which consists of an interview at the London office (£100 + VAT) or a telephone interview (£40 + VAT). A clearing house service is available to provide a shortlist of suitable schools, at a charge of £30 + VAT.

Advice is also available free of charge from Gabbitas Educational Consultants Ltd, Carrington House, 126–130 Regent Street, London W1B 5EE (tel: 020 7734 0161, fax: 020 7437 1764, website: www.gabbitas.co.uk). Gabbitas invite parents to tell them as much as possible about their child, their circumstances and the type of school they are looking for. On the basis of this information they are able to recommend a selection of suitable schools from a wide range of independent boarding and day schools. Shortlisted schools are asked to send parents a prospectus. It is then up to the parents to visit the schools personally. There is no charge for this service. Gabbitas also offer detailed guidance on education at all levels (a fee of £135 + VAT per hour is charged for such consultations).

Experienced consultants deal with a range of educational issues, including options at 16+ and planning for higher education and career opportunities.

How to choose a boarding school

Having shortlisted several schools, either with or without the guidance of a professional organisation, parents are well advised to read the prospectus through carefully, and to prepare a checklist of questions in readiness for a visit to a school.

Many of the factors governing choice are self-evident and conclusions will be arrived at quickly. Access to an international airport, proximity to relatives, religious denomination, co-educational or single-sex, the academic aims of the school and the scale of fees are points which all parents will need to consider. Also important are:

- the academic record of the school;
- the qualifications and approach of the teaching staff;
- the staff/pupil ratio;
- the physical environment;
- the attitude to discipline;
- the quality of sports education;
- the range of information technology;
- the range of extra-curricular activities;
- the quality of pastoral care;
- costs;
- the numbers in the sixth form;
- the quality of careers counselling;
- contact with parents;
- the house system;
- school publications;
- references.

Entrance examination

To be admitted to an independent secondary school your child will normally be required to pass the school's entrance test or the Common Entrance examination, which is set for candidates of 11+, 12+ and 13+ (the appropriate examination is normally determined by the child's age on 1 September in the year of entry).

- At 11+ the subjects examined are English, mathematics, science and reasoning. Examinations take place in January and November.
- At 12+ candidates sit papers in English, mathematics, science and French (written and oral). Latin may be offered as an optional paper. Examinations take place in February/March and November.
- At 13+ the papers are English, mathematics, science, French (written and oral), history, geography and religious studies. English as an additional language, German, Spanish, Latin and Greek may be offered as optional papers. Examinations take place in February/March, June (for most candidates) and November. Candidates for boys' schools most commonly take the 13+ examination.

Each senior school sets its own entrance standards and is responsible for the assessment of papers. Some schools require candidates to sit their own independent examinations in addition, or as an alternative, to Common Entrance. The examinations are normally taken at the candidate's own school.

Children applying to boarding schools from abroad or from state schools will be in direct competition with those who have been tutored for the entrance examinations at UK prep schools. Many schools will take this fact into consideration when making their assessments. However, in some cases it may be necessary to arrange individual coaching in advance of the examination. Consultancy and assessment, as well as tuition, are available from members of the Association of Tutors, Sunnycroft, 63 King Edward Road, Northampton NN1 5LY; tel: 01604 624171. Supportive tuition or complete coverage can be provided for primary and secondary work, as well as some university-level work. Some services are available on a distance basis, and some as intensive, holiday-period schemes. Examination advice and preparation for particular exams, like the Common Entrance, is a particular expertise.

The syllabuses for each subject, and the examination papers, are set by the Independent Schools Examinations Board. Copies of syllabuses, past papers and information are available from: The Independent Schools Examinations Board, Jordan House, Christchurch Road, New Milton, Hants BH25 6QJ; tel: 01425 621111, fax: 01425 620044.

Scholarships

Many independent schools offer entrance scholarships to children of outstanding ability or potential. These may be based either on general academic standard or on particular strengths, notably musical, sporting or artistic. Individual schools will supply details on request.

A number of schools offer bursaries for means-tested families. Others make specific awards to the children of clergy and service families.

ISC runs an advisory service on scholarships and bursaries for parents seeking general advice.

Insurance and financial planning

A growing number of financial service groups and independent financial advisers are able to offer school fee plans, with obvious benefits for those who are able to plan and save well in advance. For those with a more immediate requirement, loan schemes, both equity and non-equity based, are available. ISC produces a useful leaflet called *School Fees*.

Many schools cooperate with insurance companies in schemes for the remission of school fees during unavoidable absence through illness. Other policies are available that guarantee the continued payment of fees in the event of a parent's death, disablement or redundancy before the completion of schooling.

Maintained boarding schools

Some local authorities run their own boarding schools or offer boarding facilities alongside day schools. Eighteen of these maintained schools have opted out and are now grant maintained (grant maintained schools have been given a new status under government plans but this should not affect the education provided). Although any child with a legal right to attend school in Britain may seek entry to any maintained school, some authorities give priority to local children, even for boarding places. As tuition is free at these schools and parents pay only for boarding, the overall costs are approximately a half to two-thirds of the cost of an independent school. Many pupils are from service families, or have parents who work for banks or government agencies abroad.

The Guide to Accredited Independent Boarding Schools in the UK is published by the Boarding Schools Association. Copies may be obtained from them at 35–37 Grosvenor Gardens, London SW1W 0BS; tel: 020 7798 1580, fax: 020 7798 1581, website: www.boarding.org.uk or from the DCSF (website: www.dfes.gov.uk).

Local authority grants

Some education authorities are prepared to give grants to assist with boarding school fees when both parents are abroad and there are no places available in a state boarding school. Application should be made to the director of education or chief education officer for the area in the UK in which the family is normally resident.

Arrangements for your child

A boarding school accepts responsibility for the day-to-day welfare of its pupils in term-time, but overseas parents will naturally want assurance that their child is being cared for at all times, including short holiday periods and occasions when they may be in transit between school and home. There are a number of organisations that care for children in these circumstances.

Child supervision

Some boarding schools are able to send a school bus or driver to collect children from, and deliver them to, the nearest airport. Where this service is not available parents may wish to use a commercial escort service.

■ Universal Aunts Ltd, PO Box 304, London SW4 0NN (tel: 020 7738 8937) can arrange for children to be taken to and from school according to parents' instructions. They try to allot the same 'aunt' to a child so that a warm relationship is established. When required to do so they can also arrange for children to be accommodated for the night in the home of one of the aunts. Holiday accommodation is also available.

■ Corona Worldwide, c/o The Commonwealth Institute, Kensington High Street, London W8 6NQ (tel/fax: 020 7610 4407) provide a dependants' (adults and children) escort service for members.

Finding a guardian

Most boarding schools require parents to appoint a local guardian for their child. Several organisations are able to offer a guardianship service for parents who do not wish to impose upon relations or family friends.

Guardianship schemes have developed in response to demands from parents and schools to cover welfare, education and finance. They are provided by, for example, the following organisations:

- Clarendon International Education, 41 Clarendon Square, Royal Leamington Spa, Warwickshire CV32 5QZ (tel: 01926 316793, fax: 01926 883278, www.clarendon.uk.com).
- Guardians and Tutors, 131 Pomphlett Road, Plymstock, Plymouth PL6 7BU (tel: 01752 401942).
- Gabbitas Educational Consultants Ltd (www.gabbitas.co.uk) run a comprehensive guardianship service which takes care of all aspects of education, welfare and finance.
- Joanella Slattery Associates (JSA), Gilpin, Station Road, Withyham, Hartfield, East Sussex TN7 4BT (tel: 01892 770585/ 0850 943106, fax: 01892 770120, e-mail: joanella@sol.com, website: www.cea.co.uk).
- GJW Education Services, Southcote, Coreway, Sidmouth EX10 9SD (tel: 01395 512300, fax: 01395 577271, e-mail: gjweaver@netcomuk.co.uk).

Day schools in the UK

If you feel that your child is unsuited to boarding school life, or that it would be too disruptive to move schools – for example, during the GCSE years – you may wish to consider a day place. Where relatives and friends are available to care for your child this arrangement can work smoothly, particularly when a child continues at his or her present school. Many older children are reluctant to leave their friends and interests behind, and are able to respond positively to a new degree of independence.

In some cases, where there are no relatives or friends to rely on and parents wish to avoid placing their child in lodgings, mothers stay behind with their children. Although this offers the child continuity it can cause strains in the marital relationship and may offset the financial benefits of the posting.

Few employers offer more than a token allowance for lodging if your child remains at a day school in the UK.

SCHOOLS ABROAD

Neill Ransom, Chelstoke International

Expatriate schools

Unlike other nations such as France, Germany, Japan, Switzerland or the United States, Britain provides no financial assistance for the creation and management of schools for British expatriates. This means that British parents moving abroad must expect to pay substantial school fees unless they choose to send their children to local national schools.

British schools

There is a large and increasing number of 'British' schools operating in many countries of the world, the majority based in the major cities, which attract large numbers of international companies and diplomatic services.

Most of these follow the British National Curriculum (beware – as there are many similarly termed 'National Curricula'). However, also beware – in many countries one can also find 'British school' used as a name for local private schools, which provide an 'old style' English school curriculum but are populated almost entirely by local national children.

While most British schools abroad are not 'government' approved or registered and as independent organisations are not subject to Ofsted inspection, the majority of the most successful and best-performing British schools nevertheless undertake inspections or take part in recognised accreditation schemes.

There are various groups of British schools, either relating to membership of an association, such as the British Schools of the Middle East (BSME – see www.bsme.uk) or group ownership, such as the British Schools of America (currently comprising the British Schools of Washington, Boston, Chicago, Houston and Charlotte – see www.britishschools.org). The latter were set up as a direct response to British companies and staff relocating abroad and expressing concern that local schools (even where the language was similar) did not prepare their children for the British National Curriculum and any return home. Similarly, a number of British schools, for example in Eastern Europe, are currently operated by Nord Anglia, a listed UK company. In Hong Kong the well-established English Schools Foundation (www.esf.ed.hk) operates a number of high-quality primary and secondary schools and is somewhat similar to an independent LEA (Local Education Authority).

One of the best established groups, comprising individual British International Schools, is COBISEC (The Council of British Independent Schools in the European Community), comprising 35 members and 28 affiliates, from 36 countries. This group is uniquely recognised by the DfES and their teachers can join the UK teachers superannuation scheme. COBISEC has recently agreed to act jointly with FOBISSEA (The Federation of British International Schools in South and East Asia). The respective websites are www.cobisec.org and www.fobissea.org.

A small number of British schools abroad are affiliated to UK professional associations including HMC (the Headmasters' and Headmistresses' Conference), GSA (the Girls' Schools Association) and NAHT (the National Association of Headteachers). These and other links allow headteachers and staff to keep abreast of UK educational developments.

The European Schools

Starting with the first European School established in Luxembourg in 1953, there are now 12 European Schools situated in Luxembourg, Belgium (Brussels I, Brussels II, Brussels III and MoI), Germany (Karlsruhe, Munich and Frankfurt), Italy (Varese), The Netherlands (Bergen), the UK (Culham, near Oxford) and Spain (Alicante).

Linked to and supported by the European Commission, this network of schools enjoys government and Community support. A particular feature of the education provided is the European Baccalaureate, specially established for this group of schools.

US schools

US schools offer a US curriculum, but may be an option for British children because the language of instruction is English. It is important to remember that the educational approach will be quite different and that pupils will be prepared for US examinations at college entry level, such as the Standard Achievement Tests (SATs). To graduate from a US school a certain number of credits are required. Credit courses in the final two years of schooling may

Home Schooling with the World-wide Education Service

Expatriate families face many decisions when they relocate to another country and one of the most important considerations is ensuring their children receive a good education. An increasingly popular option is home schooling and the World-wide Education Service is one of the leading providers in this field. It was founded more than 100 years ago and over the last twenty-five years the service has focused on children living abroad aged 4-14. Children following **WES** courses can be found all over the world from the relative comfort of a Western European country to a remote village in Africa, a war torn country, a Pacific island or even on board a yacht!

The programme of individually selected courses creates an environment where parents teach their own children, backed by a full range of books and materials. They also have the help, support and guidance of a personal tutor, who regularly monitors and reports on each child's progress. The one to one teaching situation allows a child's individual needs, experience and potential to be developed in a settled and happy atmosphere. Special needs children often blossom in home school and coursework can be adapted to accommodate individual requirements. **WES** courses guide parents through their children's lessons in a logical and straightforward way and are designed for non-teachers to follow with ease. The package offers the perfect solution for parents who travel frequently and prefer to have their children accompany them. It gives parents flexibility to take short-term contracts while ensuring the continuity of their children's education. Unlike internet based home schools, parents can manage daily schedules to meet their own needs. They are also fully aware of what their children are learning and parent and child find this a mutually rewarding experience. A "top-up service" where parents can combine enrolment at a local school with **WES** courses in other subjects is also available.

WES courses are accredited by the Open Distance Learning Quality Council and are in line with the National Curriculum of England so children can slot back into UK or International schools with ease.

Whatever the future holds home schooling can play a valuable part – it is not only worthwhile and enjoyable but provides a unique and everlasting experience for all the family.

WORLD-WIDE EDUCATION SERVICE
PARENTS DID YOU KNOW THERE IS AN ALTERNATIVE TO LOCAL AND BOARDING SCHOOLS?

The **World-wide Education Service (WES) Home School** enables parents to teach their children at home either on a full time or 'top-up' basis.

Courses are in line with the **National Curriculum of England** and tailored to children's individual needs.

Accredited by the Open Distance Learning Quality Council (ODL QC)

WES offers:

- Courses in English, Mathematics Science and Humanities from 4-14

- Single subjects to complement local schooling

- Daily lesson plans

- Tutorial support, advice and assessment

- Educational books and materials

- Easy to follow courses which require no previous teaching experience

- Courses which can be started at any time of the year

WES Home School – proven and used by families throughout the world

For further details contact Alison Mullock at WES Home School, Waverley House, Penton, Carlisle, Cumbria CA6 5QU UK
Tel:44 (0) 1228 577123   Fax:44 (0)1228 577333
www. weshome.demon.co.uk   E-Mail:office@weshome.demon.co.uk

include Honours and Advanced Placement Sections which provide able students with special challenges. British universities are familiar with the entrance requirements of leading US universities and set similar entry requirements for applicants from US-style schools.

International schools

International schools are established in most capital cities of the world. They may be distinguished by the fact that they are independent of any state system and aim to educate children from a variety of nationalities.

Many are outstanding, offering intellectual pluralism and exceptional cultural variety – typically 50 to 60 different nationalities are represented in the student body. Some are members of international associations such as the United World Colleges and the European Council of International Schools (ECIS); others have headteachers in membership of the (British-based) Headmasters' and Headmistresses' Conference or the Girls' Schools Association.

In many respects they are as varied as their locations – large or small, monolingual, bilingual (using a foreign language as a medium of instruction for some subjects) or even multilingual (using more than one foreign language as a medium of instruction), traditional or emphatically modern. Some are subsidised by local governments, others are among the most costly schools in the world. Almost all are co-educational, and in the majority the language of instruction is English.

Curriculum options

International schools may follow a standard US college preparatory programme or a standard GCSE or International GCSE (IGCSE) programme, or a combination of these. Although a number of schools also work towards national examinations such as the German Abitur or the Spanish Bachillerato, at sixth-form level many are now preparing for the diploma of the International Baccalaureate Organisation (IBO).

A few years ago, the choice of curriculum at international schools was between a US 'international' curriculum and a British 'international' curriculum. However, there is now a range of specially designed international curriculum options available, the majority of which are well established, well supported and recognised internationally. The curriculum offered can often be a determining factor in choice of school – at least where the luxury of choice exists.

The highly successful International Baccalaureate (IB) for post-16 students has led to the development of both the MYP (Middle Years Programme) and the PYP (Primary Years Programme) also administered and accredited by the International Baccalaureate Organisation (IBO) from its headquarters and offices in Geneva and Cardiff. The PYP followed by the MYP are thematic skills-based curricula, designed to lead students through to the IB and as such are gaining popularity in increasing numbers of International Schools – details on the IBO website at www.ibo.org.

The other well-established alternative at primary level is the IPC (International Primary Curriculum). This was originally developed by Fieldwork (www.fieldworkeducation.co.uk) for the worldwide Shell Group of International Schools and its success and credibility had led to its being taken up by many successful International Schools. The IPC is operated by Fieldwork Education Services (see www.international primary curriculum.com), which is now a division of World Class Learning Schools & Systems Group (www.greatlearning.com).

The alternative – and somewhat less international – option at secondary level is those schools that follow a curriculum leading to the IGCSE (International General Certificate of Secondary Education), which is a derivative of the UK GCSE.

For post-16 students, the International Baccalaureate (IB) is based on a two-year curriculum that maintains a balance between the sciences, the arts and languages. The programme is broader than A-levels as all students must offer one subject from each of six groups:

- Language A (first language)
- Language B (second language)
- Individuals and societies
- Experimental sciences
- Mathematics
- Electives (including art, music, IT).

Of the six subjects studied, three are taken at Higher level, and three at Standard level. This represents a deliberate compromise between the European emphasis on breadth and the British tradition of rigorous specialisation. In effect students offer three subjects to A level equivalent standard and three subjects to a standard somewhat above GCSE. To be eligible for the award of the Diploma candidates must score a minimum of points and meet three additional requirements: submission of an extended essay; satisfactory completion of a Theory of Knowledge Course; and compulsory participation in a CAS programme (Creativity, Action, Service).

Students holding the IB Diploma have entered more than 700 universities throughout the world. All UK universities accept the IB as satisfying their general requirement for entrance. For further information contact: The International Baccalaureate Organisation, Curriculum and Assessment Centre, Peterson House, Malthouse Avenue, Cardiff Gate, Cardiff CF23 8GL (tel: 02920 547 777, fax: 02920 547 778, website: www.ibo.org).

Another worldwide school-leaving certificate, which has been available to English-medium schools throughout the world since 1986, is the Advanced Intermediate Certificate of Education (AICE). AICE is a 'group' certificate which is awarded on the basis of a broad and balanced curriculum of five full-credit courses or their equivalent. All candidates must take at least one course from three subject groups: mathematics and sciences; languages; and arts and humanities. The AICE curriculum, which is designed to be of worldwide relevance, offers a high degree of flexibility. As there are no compulsory subjects, student programmes may range from the highly specialised to the general. Most UK universities now accept AICE as an alternative to A levels. AICE is administered by the University of Cambridge Local Examinations Syndicate (UCLES), 1 Hills Road, Cambridge CB1 2EU (tel: 01223 553311, fax: 01223 460278, website: www.ucles.org.uk).

Special Educational Needs

If your child has Special Educational Needs (SEN), then it is very important to check in detail with likely schools as very many international schools are not able to provide relevant and sufficient support for such students. This is because the support facilities and back-up agencies we rely on in the UK often do not exist abroad. It is therefore important to discuss things in detail with any possible school, so there can be no misunderstanding.

How to find an overseas school

Finding out what schools are available abroad in specific countries and cities can be done via two main routes.

The first is via the internet, where a majority of schools – especially successful international schools of every type – maintain a website presence. Indeed, many of the websites are extremely professional and give enormous insight into the life of the school. A search for schools and city/country or international schools, etc will invariably bring up some options.

However, a second and perhaps more inclusive start will be via those organisations that exist to support and advise on international schools and education abroad. The most comprehensive and best established is ECIS (European Council of International Schools), in itself a misleading name as it has now expanded to include membership schools in most countries of the world. The success of ECIS has led to the founding of a sister organisation – CIS (Council of International Schools) which, as a service organisation, deals with the regular accreditation of international schools and headteacher and staff recruitment, in parallel with ECIS which is the membership organisation for conferences and professional support and development. Websites (www.ecis.org and www.cois.org) give full details. The membership list of ECIS/CIS in their annual *International Schools Directory* is the most comprehensive list of international schools available, with the advantage of showing which are fully accredited, or in earlier stages of membership such as affiliate members. The directory is available from John Catt Educational at www.johncatt.com with an online version via the ECIS website.

Various other websites and groups give information and lists of schools, but very few are totally comprehensive and it is unclear what is being missed.

How to choose a school abroad

Depending on the city or country and its standing as a centre of international trade or diplomatic missions, there will be a degree of choice available. In smaller, developing countries, there may be only one or two appropriate schools. In the more established international cities there will be a range of schools catering for differing national and international curricula and providing healthy competition and choice. There will often also be a number of smaller private schools with names suggesting they are British or similar, when in fact they cater predominantly for local nationals. It is thus important to discover how established and successful a school is. The first step is to check whether it has

Accredited status – ideally from ECIS and associate organisations, or, for example, as an IBO accredited school.

Information from company HR departments and other colleagues may be useful, but the needs of your children and your aspirations for them may be very different. There is no substitute for actually seeing and visiting a school, to really gain a feel of its ethos and atmosphere and meet the headteacher and key staff.

For senior executives, many international companies provide the services of an educational relocation specialist as part of their HR relocation support – often using Education Relocation Associates (ERA) (www.erauk.demon.co.uk), whose contact in Egham, Surrey is via rowena@erauk.demon.co.uk. ERA can provide a similar service advising on school placements to individual families, suggesting schools available, advising on their standing and in certain cases arranging visits and providing a specialist consultant/adviser.

Preparation is important to get the most from any school visit, or seek answers to key questions. The list below may be a helpful starter:

1. Many employers pay for families to visit the country before their projected move. This gives them the opportunity to visit the available schools (it is useful to obtain prospectuses beforehand) in person, and to consider the alternatives with existing expatriate parents and organised parents' groups which are attached to the schools. However, it is important to remember that other people may have standards which do not correspond to your own.

   In many instances expatriate schools become both a community and a social centre for expatriate families. This can be a great help for incoming families.
2. It is advisable to link house-hunting with the choice of school so that transportation problems can be considered in advance.
3. By their nature, with families being moved by companies as their agreed contract period finishes, international schools experience a steady turnover of pupils – often with 25 to 30 per cent a year moving. Similarly there will be staff turnover, as two- and three-year contracts are often the norm. The best international schools will have strategies to minimise this potential disruption – so ask the question.
4. It is important to establish how schools overseas are controlled. Many schools are run by boards composed of leading figures

from the local community, including representatives from the parent body and the organisations which use the school. The latter may be relied upon to ensure that the facilities available to their employees are of a high standard.

5. Every effort should be made to meet the headteacher, who is responsible for the quality and organisation of the school. He or she will be able to tell you whether there is a waiting list for admission to the school and when you need to register your child. In some instances the waiting time for admission can be a full academic year. Other schools may be ready to accept pupils at almost any time.

6. Take time to consider the curriculum. How far does it correspond to the National Curriculum in the UK? How straightforward will it be for your child to transfer back to the UK? Try to establish how much support, both pastoral and academic, is provided for individual children, to enable them to cope with the process of transition.

7. It is important to consider the type of report and record-keeping system which is in operation in the school. How much information will be available as a record of your child's achievement at the school? Pupil profiles are particularly essential for children who move from school to school frequently.

8. The language of instruction will be of key importance to your child. Find out what kind of English is used – whether it is American, British or non-mother-tongue English. How many children and staff do not have English as a first language? Are they likely to hinder your child's progress?

9. Expatriate schools are geared to accept pupils at any stage during the school year. However, the process of transition is generally easier when pupils begin school at the start of a new term.

10. If your company does not offer an educational allowance, or pay school fees – which is increasingly the case – then your homework needs to include fee levels. School fees tend to vary with age, with secondary and post-16, where subject specialisms increase, attracting the highest fees. In London these can be up to £16,000 for the more expensive day school fees; across Europe the fee can be €16,000 or more. While the fee may be payable in local currency, many schools operate in the more stable currencies of pounds sterling or US dollars and so exchange rate fluctuation may be a consideration. In addition to the tuition fees, it is common practice to charge a

one-off registration fee and also an initial building or development fee – the latter put towards new development or buildings either planned or recently completed.

Company-sponsored schools

In more remote countries or areas where initial development is occurring, such as new oil or gas fields, there may be no schools available. In such cases some companies will sponsor and develop a school. The trend, however, is to bring in specialist operators to operate the school on their behalf. The original worldwide network of Shell Schools, for example, is now supported and, for many aspects managed, by Fieldwork Educational Services (www.fieldworkeducation.co.uk).

Local national schools

Within Europe there are significant advantages to be gained in sending your child to a local national school, not least an opportunity to acquire proficiency in another language and to absorb a new culture. Although the standard of educational provision may vary there is no doubt that in some countries, such as France and Germany, it is excellent. However, a complete immersion in another language and culture is demanding and it will depend very much on the age and ability of the children as to how successfully they can adapt.

Learning the full range of school subjects in a new language can be exacting, particularly where no provision is made for extra language tuition. Parents who do not speak the necessary language themselves must remember that they will be able to offer little advice and assistance to their child, who may feel isolated as a result.

For those on short-term contracts it is important to consider how well such a schooling will prepare children for the next stage in a UK education. Certainly, a child working towards GCSE examinations could expect to be disadvantaged. The experience may also pose difficulties for younger children returning to the UK.

Transfer into and out of school systems in other parts of the world can also pose problems. Traditional teaching methods which rely on rote learning are still applied in many developing countries, where schools are frequently ill-equipped and crowded. As education is so highly prized as a route out of poverty, expatriates will not be encouraged to supplant a local child. However, where no alternative exists, parents may need to compensate for a restricted curriculum by providing supplementary lessons at home.

Differences in attitudes to schooling are particularly marked in countries where religious and political beliefs have shaped the curriculum. Even in other parts of the English-speaking world there are fundamental differences in approach. For example, in Australia formal schooling starts at 6 and secondary education at 12.

This section has been edited and revised by Neill Ransom, Chelstoke International (tel: 07860 212109, e-mail: neill@chelstokeinternational.com).

Checklist: Your children's education

1. Consider the options in relation to your child's age, ability and personality, and in relation to the quality of education in your new location.
2. Consider whether your organisation will contribute towards your child's education.
3. Does your host country's education system bear any resemblance to your native country's?
4. If you are considering using the independent sector, what are the financial implications, particularly when you return from your assignment?
5. If your child is to go to boarding school, what arrangements can be made for a local guardian?
6. What are the local alternatives and can you speak to other expat parents to find out what educational facilities are like in your new location?
7. Are the qualifications offered by your local national or international schools compatible with your domestic ones?
8. Can you team up with other expat families to provide a home teaching group?
9. If not, will your company provide support in setting up a company school?
10. If your child has special needs, contact support agencies for advice.

9 | Health, Security and Welfare

HEALTH RISKS

Whether you are relocating to a new country by yourself or with your family, one of the most important pre-trip considerations is what health hazards might be encountered in your host country. You might feel that developed countries might not represent too many risks to a visitor. However, it is always advisable to seek expert advice, regardless of your destination. This advice should include information not only about local health risks but also about the health service and access to medical care in your host country. While the emphasis is on developing countries, travellers should also be aware that risks in non-Third World countries are still prevalent, for example the hepatitis virus in areas of Turkey, and an outbreak of diphtheria in Russia.

A useful book that can be thoroughly recommended is *Travellers' Health* by Dr Richard Dawood (published by Oxford University Press). This provides detailed information and guidance on every conceivable medical area and is essential reading before departure.

The risks to children will also need to be identified. Some illnesses, such as gastroenteritis, present a far greater risk to children than to adults and it is essential that you arm yourself with information concerning symptoms and medical treatment, such as the administration of a fluid-replacement solution. You will also need to make sure that your child's immunisations are up to date and to identify any specific vaccines that may be required. Seek advice for babies under six months who are not able to have these immunisations.

Whatever view you wake up to

AXA PPP healthcare is right there with you

For great British healthcare – worldwide – join us now and we'll give you two months' cover free

Call +44(0)1892 550817 quoting reference WA2006 or visit www.axappphealthcare.co.uk/wa

PPP HEALTHCARE

Be Life Confident

PPP HEALTHCARE

Choose your health cover wisely

For people living abroad, quality healthcare isn't a luxury – it's a necessity. State healthcare isn't always available, or may only provide the minimum level of care, and private medical treatment without any insurance cover can be extremely costly. If you're looking for cover for you and your family it can be confusing. It's vital to understand what insurers offer, so here are some points you may wish to consider.

Will they settle my claims directly with the hospital?
Paying up front will leave you out-of-pocket after your medical treatment. To help relieve this inconvenience AXA PPP healthcare has arrangements with over 700 hospitals around the world to settle in-patient bills directly.

Speed of payment
Healthcare providers vary in the length of time they take to pay a claim, so make sure you choose a company that has a good reputation for the efficiency of its claims settlement.

The age factor?
If you're approaching retirement age check with the company that it will be able to cover you, some providers may not accept applicants over 65.

Where you live
If you take out an insurance policy that covers you for treatment whilst in a specific country or geographical area, will your medical bills be paid if you are taken ill elsewhere in the world?

How quickly can you contact your medical provider when you need them most?
Check the opening hours of customer service helplines and whether they are open at the weekends. Can you get in touch with them around the clock, 365 days a year, in case of emergency?

Customer Service Helplines

When you are living or working away from home, you need to know that any queries you have about your cover can be dealt with. Do you, for example, have access to telephone based interpretation services and facilities to help you find English speaking doctors and dentists locally?

INCLUSIONS AND EXCLUSIONS

Make sure you appreciate the scope of your cover to avoid costly misunderstandings. No insurance policy is designed to cover all eventualities so, before you buy your medical insurance policy, have you thought about:

- Being able to pre-authorise your treatment before it commences so you can be assured of your cover and, in some cases, arrange for bills to be settled directly with the hospital.

- The level of cover provided under the in-patient benefits. For example will your benefit be sufficient to pay for treatment received in the USA?

- The level of cover for day-patient and out-patient treatment: this includes procedures which don't require an overnight stay, diagnostic tests and physiotherapy. Most insurance companies vary the level of out-patient cover depending on what plan you chose.

- Parent accommodation – can you stay with your child whilst they are receiving hospital treatment?

- Emergency dental cover for accidental injury.

- Nursing at home following treatment.

- Private ambulance transportation costs.

- Cash benefit – you will receive a cash sum for each night you stay in a hospital bed when you have received free in-patient hospital treatment.

- Options for cover of pre-existing conditions and chronic conditions.

- Travel – whilst your healthcare policy should take care of your medical costs, you will also want to ensure that you have the option to be insured for any holiday and business travel outside of your area of cover.

The final point to take into consideration is that you may not see a large difference in policy and price between two insurers although the services and levels of support they offer could differ immensely. It can make all the difference to be dealing with a company who is supportive of its members, regardless of whether you need to claim on your policy or not. AXA PPP healthcare offers its members information about the countries they may travel or move to, helping to reduce the uncertainty you may feel before you arrive. General health advice and information on different illnesses or diseases you may encounter while abroad are an invaluable asset and can be available through 24-hour helplines such as Health at Hand, AXA PPP healthcare's health information line, which is staffed by healthcare professionals 365 days a year.

With over 35 years experience in the international health insurance market, AXA PPP healthcare is dedicated to looking after the healthcare insurance needs of people who are living, working or retired outside the UK for more than six months a year and in certain areas, residents residing in their home countries.

Our International Health Plan covers individuals as well as businesses of all sizes. We offer the choice of three levels of cover Standard, Comprehensive and Prestige. In addition to choosing their level of benefit, members also select an area of cover to suit their needs.

Alongside this, we have relationships with partner companies in Bahrain, Cyprus, Egypt, Malta Saudi Arabia and the United Arab Emirates, allowing us to distribute our medical insurance plans to a wide number of people worldwide.

We believe that what really makes AXA PPP healthcare different from other healthcare providers is our excellent support and service coupled with our personal touch. These are values that, alongside access to private healthcare, allow AXA PPP healthcare to give peace of mind to their members and intermediaries alike. Not only are our employees friendly, professional and efficient, they have also made it their business to help and look after you.

For further information on international health insurance from
AXA PPP healthcare please contact:
+44 1892 508 800 for individuals
+44 1892 508 795 for corporate groups
or visit **www.axappphealthcare.com**

Specialist organisations

Good general advice on health preparations before departure is available from the website of the Medical Advisory Service for Travellers Abroad (MASTA) at www.masta.org and is shown below:

- Make sure you are up to date with your immunisations such as tetanus and polio, and check which others you might need for your destination.
- Allow six to eight weeks to undergo a full course of immunisation.
- Malaria tablets should be taken one week before entering a malaria area or two to three weeks before if taking Mefloquine.
- Find out what your blood group is to ensure prompt treatment in an emergency.
- Find out how you can contact emergency services in your new location.
- If you are taking medication, make sure that you have adequate supplies and make a note of the medicines you are taking and the dosage to inform a doctor in an emergency.
- Do not take any drugs to a Third World or developing country unless they are prescribed and labelled.
- Keep a record of your medical history and briefly note down the relevant details of treatment and medication.
- Note down any pills or medicine to which you are allergic.

MASTA also offers health briefs on 230 countries. Information can be obtained direct from MASTA on 0113 238 7575, and from their Traveller's Health Line on 0906 8224100 (charged at 60p per minute). A particular feature is a personalised health brief, combining a personal medical check-up with very up-to-date information on the country (or combination of countries) to be visited, from the MASTA database, which covers more than 250 countries and includes the latest data from the Foreign Office. Central billing for companies can be arranged to cover all their employees who travel abroad. One MASTA service particularly geared to the intending expatriate is a detailed health brief and an extensive individual health report on the country concerned.

Other organisations specialising in travel medicine are as follows:

- The Malaria Reference Laboratory at the London School of Hygiene and Tropical Medicine, which runs a helpline on 09065 508908 (charged at £1 per minute).

■ The Travel Clinic, Hospital for Tropical Diseases, 4 St Pancras Way, London NW1 0PE, which offers preventative advice and has an extensive range of health products and immunisations available. For information, call their Healthline on 0839 337733; to make an appointment, telephone 020 7388 9600.

■ Only two British Airways Travel Clinics are to be found now, both in London. For details and to book appointments, call 0845 600 2236. Details are also available on the British Airways website: www.british-airways.com. The clinics offer a one-stop service, providing immunisation, health protection items such as mosquito nets and water purification tablets, and anti-malarial tablets. The British Airways Travel Clinics are affiliated to the Geneva-based international charity the Bloodcare Foundation, which can send screened and tested blood worldwide. Cover is available for individuals or families, or for a company, on a monthly or yearly basis.

There is, however, one major international health hazard that has come to the fore since earlier editions of this book: the problem of acquired immune deficiency syndrome (AIDS). It has reached epidemic proportions in some parts of Africa and other developing countries. It is no longer sufficient to warn expatriates against the dangers of promiscuity. People can become infected through transfusions of infected blood or treatment with instruments that have not been properly sterilised. Expatriates are now advised to contact the local British embassy or high commission, which keeps a register of reliable blood donors among the expatriate community. It is also inadvisable in many countries to attend local doctors' or dentists' clinics unless they are known to enforce the highest standards of hygiene. Medical kits should also be top of the packing list. Organisations such as MASTA can advise on the appropriate contents.

Those working in Saudi Arabia should note that they will have to produce a doctor's certificate to show that they are HIV negative. It has been pointed out that this can raise problems when applying for medical insurance. Even the answer 'yes' to the question 'Have you ever been HIV tested?' can raise the suspicion that your lifestyle exposes you to the risk of AIDS. Thus, if you have been HIV tested in connection with an assignment to Saudi Arabia, you should point this out if the question arises on a medical insurance form.

An extremely useful leaflet, *Travellers Guide to Health*, which covers prevention and planning, emergency care and international health care agreements, and contains an application for a European Health Insurance Card (EHIC) for free or reduced-cost emergency medical treatment in most European countries, can be obtained from your GP, or through the Health Literature Line on 0800 555 777. A comprehensive guide is available in the form of *Health Information for Overseas Travel* (published by The Stationery Office, £7.95, tel: 0870 6005522, website: www.tsonline.co.uk). This detailed work is primarily intended for reference by GPs, but serious travellers will find it most useful, as it provides a thorough guide to disease risk, immunisation and other hazards, as well as child-specific information.

EXPATRIATE MEDICAL INSURANCE

Most of the countries that expatriates go to do not operate a national health service like that of the UK. It comes as something of a shock to find oneself paying £100 or more for a routine visit to a doctor or dentist and the costs of hospitalisation can be such as to wipe out the savings of months, or even years. In places like the EU, South Africa, Australia or other developed Commonwealth countries there are established local methods of medical insurance, and in many cases the cost of this is included in the remuneration package. If not, it is certainly a matter which should be clarified while you are negotiating the job offer.

Some OPEC and similar resource-rich countries do have state medical schemes, and as a matter of fact their hospitals are, in many cases, better equipped than our relatively rundown institutions. They are, however, established primarily for the benefit of local nationals, which means that the customs and culture of medical care are different from those which most westerners are used to. For this reason, most expatriates in those countries arrange for attention in private hospitals which, needless to say, tends to be very expensive indeed. There are a lot of health legislation changes taking place in the UAE currently. People who go to the Middle East should check the health insurance legislation of each country they are going to. In Saudi Arabia and Abu Dhabi, for example, it is now required by law that employers provide all expat employees with health insurance. Medical insurance for anyone going to these places is therefore essential, and a number of plans have now been developed specifically for expatriates by AXA PPP healthcare, BUPA International and others. The health insurance business is fiercely competitive; if you are paying your own insurance you should ask your broker for a complete list of all the plans that are available, so that you can compare them in detail. You will need to establish whether quoted premiums include or exclude insurance premium tax and how long companies take to settle claims. You will also want to check that the plan you choose includes, as do AXA PPP healthcare's and BUPA International's, the typical health services that every expat has come to expect, such as medical evacuation, 24-hour helpline, translation services and arranging for direct payment in nearly every hospital throughout the world.

AXA PPP healthcare

AXA PPP healthcare is one of the longest established and largest medical insurers in Britain and has nearly 2 million customers worldwide. Its International Health Plan has three different levels of cover, of which the benefits are detailed in Table 9.1 (see page 139):

■ **Prestige.** A top of the range plan, providing all the benefits of AXA PPP healthcare's comprehensive and standard options but with the addition of routine pregnancy cover, adult health screen, disability compensation cover and annual travel insurance.
■ **Comprehensive.** As the name suggests, the plan provides comprehensive cover, in-patient, day-patient and out-patient treatment and, in addition, covers non-routine dental treatment.
■ **Standard.** A plan specifically designed for members who do not require out-patient cover but which offers similar in-patient and day-patient treatment cover to the comprehensive option.

Depending on where you reside, travel to or wish to receive treatment there are three geographical areas of cover:

■ Area 1 – worldwide;
■ Area 2 – worldwide except the United States and Canada;
■ Area 3 – Europe and specified countries.

AXA PPP healthcare defines Europe as: Albania, Andorra, Armenia, Austria, Azerbaijan, Belarus, Belgium, Bosnia and Herzegovina, Bulgaria, Channel Islands, Croatia, Republic of Cyprus (including Akrotiri and Dhekelia SBAs), Czech Republic, Denmark, Estonia, Faroe Islands, Finland, France, Georgia, Germany, Gibraltar, Greece, Greenland, Hungary, Iceland, Ireland, Isle of Man, Italy, Kazakhstan,

Table 9.1 AXA PPP healthcare – summary benefits table

The three options you can choose from	Prestige	Comprehensive	Standard
Policy benefit limit	Up to £1,250,000 each year	Up to £1,000,000 each year	Up to £750,000 each year
In-patient and day-patient treatment including surgeons', anaesthetists', physicians' and consultants' charges, diagnostic tests and physiotherapy	No annual maximum	No annual maximum	No annual maximum
Out-patient surgical procedures	No annual maximum	No annual maximum	No annual maximum
Radiotherapy, chemotherapy, computerised tomography, magnetic resonance imaging and positron emission tomography (brain and body scanning). Received as an in-patient, day-patient or out-patient	No annual maximum	No annual maximum	No annual maximum
Parent accommodation. Charges for one parent staying with a child member under 18	No annual maximum	No annual maximum	No annual maximum
International emergency treatment (evacuation or repatriation service)	No annual maximum	No annual maximum	No annual maximum
Outside area of cover. Emergency treatment, or treatment of a medical condition that arises suddenly whilst outside your area of cover.	Up to 10 weeks' treatment in any year	Up to six weeks' treatment in any year	Up to six weeks' treatment in any year
Separate limit for United States/Canada	£20,000	£15,000	£10,000

Table 9.1   *continued*

The three options you can choose from	Prestige	Comprehensive	Standard
Dental care. We will pay up to 50% of the costs incurred. The maximum we will pay in a year is:	Area 1 £600 Area 2 £500 Area 3 £400	Area 1 £400 Area 2 £320 Area 3 £240	Area 1 £400 Area 2 £320 Area 3 £240
Accidental damage to teeth	Up to £10,000 each year	Up to £10,000 each year	Up to £10,000 each year
Cash benefits for each night you receive free in-patient treatment	£100 a night	£100 a night	£100 a night
Ambulance transport for emergency transport to or between hospitals	Up to £500 each year	Up to £500 each year	Up to £500 each year
Health at Hand	Included	Included	Included
Doctor, dental, optical helpline	Included	Included	Included
Interpretation service helpline	Included	Included	Included
The International Travel Plan	Included	Optional	Optional
Out-patient treatment i) Medical practitioner charges for consultations ii) Consultations and treatment for psychiatric illness iii) Complementary practitioner charges		Complementary practitioner charges limited to £300 each year	Complementary practitioner charges limited to £300 each year
iv) Diagnostic tests and physiotherapy v) Travel and childhood vaccinations administered by a medical practitioner			
Combined overal limit Excess per visit (applying to i, ii and iii only)	£5,000 per year Nil	£3,000 per year £20	

Table 9.1 *continued*

The three options you can choose from	Prestige	Comprehensive	Standard
Hospital-at-home	Up to 28 days each year	Up to 14 days each year	
Day-patient radiotherapy and chemotherapy cash benefit	£50 a day	£50 a day	£50 a day
Out-patient drugs and dressings prescribed by a medical practitioner	Up to £500 each year	Up to £200 each year	
Optical cover	Up to £100 each year	Up to £100 each year	
Eyesight test cover	Paid in full for one eyesight test each year	Paid in full for one eyesight test each year	
Adult health screen	Up to £300 each year towards a health screen for each adult on the policy		
Disability compensation cover	Up to £50,000		
Pregnancy and childbirth (after 10 months' cover)	Up to £4,000		

Kyrgyzstan, Latvia, Liechtenstein, Lithuania, Luxembourg, FYR Macedonia, Malta, Moldova, Monaco, Netherlands, Norway, Poland, Portugal (including Madeira), Romania, Russian Federation, San Marino, Serbia and Montenegro, Slovak Republic, Slovenia, Spain, Sweden, Switzerland, Tajikistan, Turkey, Turkish Republic of Northern Cyprus, Turkmenistan, Ukraine, United Kingdom of Great Britain and Northern Ireland, Uzbekistan and Vatican City State.

As well as the private healthcare aspect of its plans, AXA PPP healthcare also gives members access to its overseas evacuation or repatriation service, which provides emergency medical advice and assistance worldwide, 24 hours a day, 365 days a year.

BUPA International

All the essential services are, of course, also provided by BUPA International, the largest specialist health insurers for expatriates, with a vast network of participating hospitals and clinics worldwide. BUPA has over 8 million members in 190 countries of 115 nationalities and can pay claims in up to 80 different currencies. BUPA International also offers its members its 'Membersworld' online service available across the range of territories covered. The benefits available under each of BUPA International's three levels of Lifeline cover are summarised in Table 9.2 (see page 144). Current premium rates, which have changed recently, will be quoted on application.

Another firm which issues its clients with a card is International SOS Assistance, whose medical and security schemes enable the holder, or those looking after him or her, to call for medical assistance at six main centres throughout the world. They specialise in emergency medical evacuation to the nearest high-quality medical facility, repatriation and return of mortal remains. AXA PPP, BUPA, Goodhealth Worldwide, Expacare, IPH, William Russell, Carecard International and other private insurers use these services. As they point out, it is only of limited use to have cover for repatriation unless it can be implemented easily. GESA Assistance provides a similar service to, among others, Falcon Healthcare.

Catering particularly for the retired expatriate, the Exeter Friendly Society does not automatically increase premium rates with advancing age, making their policies a good buy for the over-50s.

John Wason (Insurance Brokers) Ltd, founded by a former expatriate, offers a specialist 'Overseas Personal Insurance' scheme, which includes optional medical and personal accident/sickness cover worldwide. Levels of cover accord with 'units' purchased.

Finally, there is the possibility of free, or subsidised, local medical care courtesy of a reciprocal agreement with the UK health authorities. The EU and many other countries have such agreements, but the terms do vary. An EHIC is required and can be obtained from the Post Office, through the Health Literature Line on 0845 606 2030, or online via www.dh.gov.uk (your NHS or national insurance number will be required). However, this scheme is no substitute for a good insurance policy.

Some of the questions you should ask about your medical cover are as follows:

expacare
GLOBAL HEALTHCARE AND ASSISTANCE

A life abroad?
We'll help you make the most of it.

FLEXIBLE PLANS

RANGE OF BENEFITS

You lead an international lifestyle, so it makes sense that your health is taken care of by a private medical insurance provider with an international reputation.

Expacare's wide range of products and benefits are designed to make your life easy and provide peace of mind. We also know that no two individuals are the same, which is why our international medical cover is both flexible and offers a host of benefits to meet your specific needs. For those who require cover on an affordable budget or those who require more extensive cover and a wide range of benefits, rest assured with Expacare, you are in good company.

We're here to help, call

+44 (0) 1344 381 650
or visit www.expacare.com

Expacare Limited
Authorised and Regulated by the Financial Services Authority. Registered Office: 6 Crutched Friars, London EC3N 2PH.
Registered in England No 01524095. VAT No. 244 2321 96

Table 9.2   BUPA International

Summary Benefit Table

Overall annual maximum

£ Sterling
$ US Dollar
€ Euro

Out-patient treatment

Out-patient *surgical operations*

Wellness - mammogram. PAP test, prostate cancer screening or colon
cancer screening (after one year's membership)

Physiotherapy, osteopathy and chiropractor *treatment*

Costs for *treatment* by *therapists* and *complementary medicine practitioners*

Consultants' fees and *psychologists'* fees for *psychiatric treatment*
(after two years' membership)

Pathology, x-ray and *diagnostic tests*

Consultants' fees for consultations

Costs for *treatment* by a *family doctor*

Prescribed drugs and dressings

Accident-related dental *treatment*

In-patient treatment

Hospital accommodation
Surgical operations, including pre- and post-operative care
Nursing care, drugs and surgical dressings
Physicians' fees
Theatre charges and *intensive care*
Pathology, x-rays, *diagnostic tests* and physiotherapy
Prostheses and *appliances*
Parent accommodation
Psychiatric treatment (after two years membership)

Further benefits

Cancer *treatment*

Maternity cover (after 10 months membership)

MRI, CT and PET scans
Transplant Services
Local Road Ambulance

Local Air Ambulance

Home nursing after *in-patient treatment*

In-patient cash benefit

HIV/AIDS drug therapy including ART (after five years' membership)

Hospice and palliative care

In-patient rehabilitation

Newborn Care (90 days following birth)

Healthline services

Optional benefits (if purchased)

USA cover

Assistance cover

Essential	Classic	Gold
£500,000	£750,000	£1,000,000
$1,000,000	$1,500,000	$2,000,000
€750,000	€1,000,000	€1,500,000
Paid in full	Paid in full	Paid in full
Not covered	We pay up to £sterling 500, US$ 1,000 or €Euro 750 each *membership year*	We pay up to £sterling 500, US$ 1,000 or €Euro 750 each *membership year*
Not covered	We pay in full for up to 15 visits each *membership year*	We pay in full for up to 30 visits each *membership year*
Not covered	We pay in full for up to 5 visits each *membership year*	We pay in full for up to 15 visits each *membership year*
Not covered	We pay in full for up to 15 visits each *membership year*	We pay in full for up to 30 visits each *membership year*
Not covered	We pay up to £sterling 5,000, US$ 10,000 or €Euro 8000 each *membership year*	Paid in full
Not covered		Paid in full up to 35 visits
Not covered	Not covered	
Not covered	Not covered	We pay up to £sterling 600, US$ 1,200 or €Euro 900 each *membership year*
Not covered	Not covered	We pay up to £sterling 400, US$ 800 or €Euro 600 each *membership year*
Paid in full	Paid in full	Paid in full
Paid in full	Paid in full	Paid in full
Not covered	We pay up to £sterling 3,000, US$ 6,000 or €Euro 4,500 each *membership year*	We pay up to £sterling 5,000, US$ 10,000 or €Euro 7,500 each *membership year*
Paid in full	Paid in full	Paid in full
We pay up to £sterling 5,000, US$ 10,000 or €Euro 7,300 each *membership year*	We pay up to £sterling 5,000, US$ 10,000 or €Euro 7,300 each *membership year*	We pay up to £sterling 5,000, US$ 10,000 or €Euro 7,300 each *membership year*
We pay up to £sterling 100, US$ 200 or €Euro 150 each day up to a maximum of 10 days each *membership year*	We pay up to £sterling 100, US$ 200 or €Euro 150 each day up to a maximum of 20 days each *membership year*	We pay up to £sterling 100, US$ 200 or €Euro 150 each day up to a maximum of 30 days each *membership year*
We pay up to £sterling 75, US$ 150 or €Euro 110 each day up to a maximum of 20 days each *membership year*	We pay up to £sterling 75, US$ 150 or €Euro 110 each day up to a maximum of 20 days each *membership year*	We pay up to £sterling 75, US$ 150 or €Euro 110 each day up to a maximum of 20 days each *membership year*
Not covered	We pay up to £sterling 10,000, US$ 20,000 or €Euro 15,000 each *membership year*	We pay up to £sterling 10,000, US$ 20,000 or €Euro 15,000 each *membership year*
We pay up to £sterling 20,000, US$ 40,000 or €Euro 30,000 for the whole of your membership	We pay up to £sterling 20,000, US$ 40,000 or €Euro 30,000 for the whole of your membership	We pay up to £sterling 20,000, US$ 40,000 or €Euro 30,000 for the whole of your membership
We pay in full for up to 30 nights each *membership year*	We pay in full for up to 30 nights each *membership year*	We pay in full for up to 30 nights each *membership year*
We pay £sterling 75,000 US$ 150,000 or €Euro 110,000 maximum benefit for all *treatment* received during the first 90 days following birth	We pay £sterling 75,000 US$ 150,000 or €Euro 110,000 maximum benefit for all *treatment* received during the first 90 days following birth	We pay £sterling 75,000 US$ 150,000 or €Euro 110,000 maximum benefit for all *treatment* received during the first 90 days following birth
Included	Included	Included
100% of costs in network. 80% of costs out of network provided *treatment* is pre-authorised. Only 50% of *treatment* costs if you do not pre-authorise	100% of costs in network. 80% of costs out of network provided *treatment* is pre-authorised. Only 50% of *treatment* costs if you do not pre-authorise	100% of costs in network. 80% of costs out of network provided *treatment* is pre-authorised. Only 50% of *treatment* costs if you do not pre-authorise

See section 4 for details of the optional Assistance cover. Your Membership Certificate will show if you have purchased this cover. The overall annual maximum benefit limit does not apply.

International Medical Insurance as individual as you are.

At Expacare, we realise the importance of your health and wellbeing while working abroad.

We also know that no two individuals are the same, which is why our international medical cover is both flexible and offers a range of benefits designed to meet your specific needs.

Expacare are committed to providing you with the right solution and delivering a service beyond your expectations, if your circumstances change, so too can your cover. After all, your peace of mind is our business.

We are always looking at new and innovative ways of satisfying the needs of our clients. That's why with all Expacare plans comes a dedicated point of contact to take care of your policy administration as well as access to regional specific products. You can also benefit from a wide network of participating hospitals, doctors and local clinics, so you know you'll always be in safe hands.

Rest assured with Expacare, you are in good company. We are one of the longest established international healthcare insurers with over 30 year's experience in providing cover for individuals of all nationalities in over 140 countries worldwide.

We pride ourselves in offering a wide range of healthcare insurance solutions and a host of benefits suitable for a variety of requirements:

- Basecare
- Standardcare
- Executivecare
- Specialcare

For those who require cover on an affordable budget, our Basecare plan offers the ideal option for individuals looking for key areas of cover. For more extensive cover and a full range of benefits, our Select range of products include a choice of 3 key cover plans including: Standardcare, Executivecare and Specialcare. In addition to our Select range of products we also offer Mediksure and Momentum plans for specific regions of cover.

We're here to help, for more information on Expacare's flexible plans and benefits call
+44 (0) 1344 381 650
or visit www.expacare.com

Expacare Limited. Authorised and Regulated by the Financial Services Authority. Registered Office: 6 Crutched Friars, London EC3N 2PH.   Registered in England No 01524095.

1. Does the scheme cover all eventualities?
2. Are the scheme's benefits realistic in the light of local costs?
3. Can you make claims immediately or is there an initial indemnity period during which claims are disallowed? (Some insurers insist on this to protect themselves from claims caused by 'pre-existing medical conditions'.)
4. Is there a clause providing for emergency repatriation by air, or air ambulance, if suitable treatment is not available locally? If so, who decides what constitutes an emergency and/or adequate local treatment?
5. Is the insurer's nearest office accessible personally or by telephone?
6. What is the length of the insurer's settlement period for claims?
7. Is there a discount for members of professional or other associations?
8. Does the policy continue to apply, partly or fully, while you are back in the UK?
9. What is the insurer's attitude to AIDS and HIV tests?

PERSONAL SECURITY

There are overseas countries where crimes against persons, either for gain or to make political points, are a serious hazard. Countries where Islamic fundamentalism is rampant are a case in point. Other places, notably in Africa and Latin America, qualify as high-risk locations in terms of personal safety, eg Colombia, Zimbabwe, Brazilian cities and Johannesburg. There are also corporate or national connections that may be the target of terrorists:

- Anything to do with Israel. It is still advisable to carry a separate passport if you have a visa for Israel but also travel to the Middle East.
- Employees of companies associated with pollution, nuclear waste and animal experiments.
- Nationals of countries that have recently been, or are currently, in serious dispute with countries in which an expatriate is living – or even its allies.

According to the international security consultants Merchants International Group (MIG), resident expatriates tend to be more at risk in these circumstances than visiting businessmen. However, the terrorist attacks on the World Trade Center in New York and the

Bupa International –
The World Health Service

Every year over 200,000 Britons move overseas to live or work – and while the experience is exciting, for many it can also represent a challenge, with so much to plan and think about, from finding the right accommodation to learning the local language. Make sure if you are moving abroad this year that you don't forget to prioritise your health – as healthcare systems overseas can vary enormously from the UK, even if you are staying within Europe. International private medical insurance can provide you and your family with the peace of mind you need when it comes to health and care – as getting ill abroad can be no joke.

Bupa International, part of the British owned Bupa Group, has been caring for the healthcare needs of expats and their families around the globe for over 35 years. We understand that expats want peace of mind about their health while abroad – and a health insurer they can rely on to provide a high quality service and comprehensive coverage. That is why we are the largest expatriate insurer in the world, covering over 720,000 people in 190 countries, with a range of high quality and flexible insurance products, designed for groups and individual's living and working abroad.

As one of the pioneers of the international private medical insurance market, Bupa International leads the way in the benefits it provides it customers, including access to:

- A worldwide network of over 5,500 participating hospitals
- Specialist doctors who are trained in emergency and aviation medicine
- Bupa International's 24-hour helpline, open 365 days a year, which is manned by a team of experienced advisers who, between them, speak 34 languages.

This is all backed up by benefits such as direct settlement of bills, fast claims turnaround – Bupa International processes 10,000 claims a week – and local knowledge on a global scale, which ensures that we offer protection and support for people living and working anywhere in the world.

Flexibility is also the hallmark of private medical insurance from Bupa International, with customers enjoying flexible benefits such as primary care cover, maternity cover, home nursing, routine and emergency dentistry, as well as hospital treatment and accommodation, health checks, emergency road ambulance and cover for sports injuries. Bupa International also leads the way in innovation and has just increased its cover for chronic diseases, such as diabetes and asthma, beyond diagnosis to include treatment, including drugs and consultations. As chronic conditions become more common across the globe, the benefit this move provides our customers cannot be underestimated from both a financial perspective and the peace of mind this extended cover provides.

Top tips when choosing international private medical insurance:

1. Consider the experiences of people who have already moved abroad – their insider advice can be invaluable.

2. Make sure you choose a scheme that suits your needs, circumstances and budget.

3. Choose an insurer that can offer you advice and support on medical facilities in the country you are moving to.

4. Consider whether you would like to be covered for emergency evacuation and repatriation – if you are moving to a less developed country this is vital so that you can be sure to get the medical treatment you need.

5. Make sure your insurer is there for you around the clock – look for a 24 hour helpline, which can answer your questions on everything from inoculations to visa requirements.

For more information about Bupa International's insurance policies go to:
www.bupa-intl.com

Pentagon in Washington of 11 September 2001 and the rigorous new entry checks and routines that the United States has introduced on all incoming airline passengers have brought to the forefront the constant risks from terrorism to which all business travellers are exposed, even in the most developed countries. The same is, of course, true for visitors to European cities, as the London bombing incidents in July 2005 demonstrated. MIG, which speculates in the 'grey areas' of risk often associated with developing countries, is available for advice on these matters. For more information, visit the MIG website at www.merchantinternational.com. Since 11 September 2001 it seems less likely that the chances of winning the lottery jackpot are higher than that of being anywhere near a terrorist attack.

ACCIDENTS

Finally, it is worth sounding a note of warning. In many countries getting involved in legal action can be disastrous – even when it is over a minor incident. It is certainly worth researching your host country's attitude to such events and what kind of ethical stance it takes on such matters – including that of bribery. Check if your company has an ethical policy on such matters.

In some parts of the world it might be wise to hire a driver rather than take the risk of getting involved in an accident yourself. It is important not to take any unnecessary risks, as many countries are unsympathetic to practices accepted as normal in other parts of the world, such as drinking alcohol or gambling.

Checklist: Health, security and welfare

1. Avoid daily routines, like taking the same route to work every day at a fixed time.
2. Remove bushes and thick vegetation around the entrance to your house or place of work – they could make a hiding place for criminals and people tend to be least vigilant as they approach familiar places.
3. If you think you are being followed, head immediately for a place where there are as many other people around as possible. Criminals prefer not to strike when there are witnesses about.

5. Watch out for abandoned cars in the vicinity. These are sometimes dumped by criminals to test police vigilance.
6. Avoid conspicuous displays of affluence.
7. Try to have a room in your house to which you and your family can retreat if serious danger threatens. It should have good doors with stout locks, and windows that can be secured from the inside but which do not bar escape routes. If possible, get professional advice on how to prepare what is called a 'keep' in your house.
8. Using firearms as a form of self-defence is fraught with danger. You will nearly always be faced with more than one assailant and you have to be prepared to shoot to kill. That in itself is much less easy than it is made to look in the movies; furthermore, in some countries foreigners are always in the wrong in such circumstances.
9. The best form of defence and survival is to rehearse a plan of action in your mind in case you are attacked or in danger – and to stick to it if you can. The thing to avoid above all is panic, because if you panic you lose control of the situation.

10 Adjusting to Living and Working Abroad

Living and working overseas can be extremely rewarding in personal, financial and career terms. It is also likely to herald a dramatic change of lifestyle. All expatriates, no matter to which country they are posted, have to make some adjustment to life overseas, and all members of an expatriate's family will be affected by the move, whether or not they venture abroad. If, as a married person, you go abroad 'on unaccompanied status', you and your family will have to make a number of adjustments to living separately. There is much to be gained in going abroad as a couple, but in so doing you may be asking your partner to give up a career and possible future chances of employment, and, if you have children, disrupting their education, and removing your family from their normal sources of comfort and support (see Chapters 7 and 8).

For families who do decide to relocate together, a failure to adapt might mean having to terminate the contract early. Such unscheduled returns to the UK tend to cause considerable disturbance and hardship to all concerned. There is a high turnover rate among expatriates, so before you commit yourself and your family to working abroad it is important to discuss the likely consequences of the move with other members of your family.

CULTURE SHOCK

In contemplating a move overseas you have probably tried to imagine what it will be like. Most people think about the physical differences:

the heat, the humidity, the dirt, etc, although they are rarely able to assess how these differences will affect their daily lives. How will working in 90 per cent humidity impair your effectiveness? Could you negotiate an important contract in an atmosphere more suited to the tropical house of your nearest botanical gardens? It is difficult to appreciate how much of the background to daily life is taken for granted; for example, drinking water from a tap, flicking a switch for light, pushing a button for instant entertainment. In underdeveloped countries many of these basics of everyday life either do not exist or function irregularly. While it is easy to imagine that things will be different, it is hard to envisage how this affects the quality of daily life and your sense of well-being.

But the differences that prove the greatest barrier to adjustment are the ones that cannot be seen and that are not normally even thought about. Despite regional differences in the UK most people have grown up with common experiences and expectations of how the world works. In any given situation, most people have a fairly clear idea of what is expected of them and what they expect of others. However, different nationalities do not necessarily share the same assumptions and expectations about life, or about how other people should behave. In Britain we share a common culture and, on the whole, common beliefs about what is right and proper. Other cultures, though, have quite different underlying values and beliefs, different expectations and concepts of 'normal behaviour'. Britain is nominally a Christian country, yet although much legislation and ordinary behaviour have their origins in Christian teaching, a relatively small proportion of the population would see Christianity as the driving force of British society.

By contrast, in Saudi Arabia, Islam underlies everything. It regulates the legal and political system and the conduct of all aspects of everyday life and is so perceived by its own nationals. It can be difficult to understand how other people operate; it is easy to assume that the motivations of others are understood, while misunderstanding them utterly. In Britain the ground rules of human behaviour can be taken for granted, but overseas they must be questioned and come to terms with. For example, in Malaysia it is not uncommon for expatriates to feel that their local subordinates are disloyal when, instead of discussing some decision with which they disagree, they simply choose to ignore it. Yet to the Malaysian it would be unpardonable to cause a superior to lose face by questioning him in public; far more polite simply to ignore what is considered to be a poor suggestion. Even unconscious behaviour is open to misinterpretation. For example, in the UK an individual who avoids eye contact would usually be categorised (unconsciously) as shifty or guilty. In Nigeria the same individual would be seen as respectful, because to avoid eye contact with an older person is a mark of respect. The classic example of how the smallest physical cues are subject to different interpretations is one of distance. The British tend to feel comfortable standing two to three feet apart when chatting; the Saudis prefer to stand closer together. A Saudi and a Briton talking to each other will each unconsciously try to establish the distance at which each feels comfortable. The Briton will feel threatened when the Saudi edges nearer and the Saudi will feel rebuffed as the Briton sidles backwards. Neither will appreciate the impact of his or her unconscious behaviour on the other. This kind of disorientation is experienced constantly by the fledgling expatriate, causing many expatriates to respond aggressively when no hostility was intended.

The expatriate experiences considerable anxiety when faced unknowingly with the loss of minor cues: the familiar signs and symbols that are taken for granted in the UK but are open to different interpretations in the host country. This constant disorientation is unnerving and can cause considerable stress. The syndrome is so common that it has been given a name – culture shock.

Doctors have long recognised that changes in normal lifestyle can result in stress, and ultimately physical and mental illness. Change of home, change of friends, change of job, change of lifestyle, loss of or separation from the marital partner may all be experienced by the expatriate, who may be deprived of his or her traditional means of support and solace. A new job is always stressful, but when the job is in a new (and seemingly hostile) environment, the tensions are even greater. Symptoms associated with culture shock include heightened anxiety and worry, feelings of isolation and helplessness, and a poor performance at work. Most expatriates eventually settle down, more or less successfully, but there is a predictable cycle to the adjustment and three main stereotyped responses to adaptation.

First, there is the chauvinistic expatriate, whose response to his or her predicament is to try to create a mini encapsulated UK or 'Little England'. This expatriate's attempts to understand the local way of doing things, or local colleagues, are minimal. Faced with the difficulties of this new environment he or she retreats from what is perceived as a hostile host country and people. The blame for misunderstandings is never anything to do with him or her, but is always the fault of the 'stupid' locals. This expatriate falls into a trap of denigrating everything local and idealising everything from home, ultimately provoking real hostility from local counterparts and making a reality of his or her view of him- or herself alone against the world. Local expatriate clubs are full of this kind of expatriate, who often indulges his or her aggression over more drinks than are healthy.

The chauvinistic expatriate is experiencing culture shock. He or she is disorientated by the environment and feels constantly at sea. The symptoms of this state are incessant complaining, glorification of the UK, alcoholic over-indulgence, marital difficulties and general aggression. At this stage the expatriate will find it hard to work with local colleagues or clients and will be permanently miserable. It is at this stage also that expatriates tend to terminate their contracts, prior to completion, with major repercussions for their families and their own careers. Fortunately for most expatriates, this is a passing stage and after their first home leave, when the realities of life in Britain are forced upon them, they manage to adapt successfully.

The second, much rarer, response is to 'go bush'. This expatriate eschews the company of his fellow expatriates, and tends to over-idealise all things local. He identifies totally with the host culture, which many of his local colleagues find both patronising and suspect.

The third and probably most appropriate response, but the most difficult to achieve, is that of the 'open-minded expatriate' who, without abandoning his or her own values, is able to accept the new culture and attempt to understand it. This involves understanding how the host society's values are reflected in everyday behaviour. Decisions are made without the necessity for qualitative judgement. While differences are acknowledged, they are not categorised as better or worse.

If, prior to arriving abroad, you can come to terms with the idea that there are real cultural differences which need to be understood, you will find it much easier to adjust. These cultural differences affect work and home life. Often at work the differences are hidden because on the surface the work to be done is the same as at home, but local colleagues may have different ways of doing business and different attitudes to time and concepts of loyalty. Management styles may differ and motivation and discipline have quite different connotations. For example, many other nationalities find Western haste in business negotiations unpalatable; it is good manners and a useful way of assessing a business associate to chat seemingly inconsequentially before getting down to real negotiations. The Westerner considers it a waste of time, even insulting. In many parts of the world ethnic loyalty is a salient feature of everyday life, and a member of one tribe may be under an obligation to find jobs not only for his extended family, ie sons and daughters of aunts, uncles, cousins, and children of his father's other wives, but also for members of his own ethnic group. Outside the West, age is still considered to bestow authority and seniority, even at work. Social adjustment can also be difficult. Business is often conducted at social events; business entertaining at home may be the norm. Social life can be restricted, as in many areas expatriates make little attempt to get to know local people and mix almost entirely in expatriate circles. This can cause considerable pressure, as any minor upset at work or at home is common knowledge and long remembered.

The married expatriate living alone abroad often has the most difficulty in adjusting, both when working and when on leave. Single people often feel excluded from much social activity which revolves around the family. Single women suffer especially, as other expatriate women may resent or even fear them, and friendship with local colleagues can be misinterpreted. However, it is often the partners who bear the brunt of culture shock and have the greatest difficulty in adapting, as discussed in a previous chapter.

PREPARING YOURSELF FOR THE CHANGE

So how can you, as a prospective expatriate, prepare yourself and your family to make the appropriate adjustments? First, you and your family should try to find out as much as possible about the country before you accept the assignment, and preferably before you go to the job interview. Once you have accepted a job offer, some employers will give you a briefing of some description. Relatively few employers seem to appreciate that the cost of staff turnover, in money, time, effort and damage to relationships with their clients, merits an outlay on briefing expatriates and their families before their departure.

You will need to know something about your employer, the nature and responsibilities of your job, the terms and conditions of your contract and whether the benefits offered match the prevailing conditions in the country. You will want to learn about the country, its history, geography, climate, politics, economics, form of government, people and religion, etc. Much of this basic or factual information will be available in standard publications from the national embassies and tourist offices (although most countries naturally like to present a favourable picture of themselves). There are a number of specialised directories available in public reference libraries containing this information and some banks, such as HSBC, produce factual booklets. The DTI produces a vast range of publications aimed at business abroad, many of which contain information of value to intending expatriates. A full list is provided in the Export Publications Catalogue, available FOC from DTI Export Publications, Admail 528, London SW1W 8YT; tel: 020 7510 0171, fax: 020 7510 0197, as well as details of other services. Your local Government Office or Business Link is another source of information linked to the DTI. Corona Worldwide produces its own *Notes for Newcomers* which contains background on each country with advice on setting up home.

The financial problems of expatriate life, such as personal taxation, insurance, etc, and other aspects of interest to expatriates are covered in several magazines catering specifically for their needs, available on subscription:

- *Nexus* (monthly), annual subscription rates £66 for the UK, £72 for Europe and £78 for the rest of the world, published by Expat Network, 1st Floor, 5 Brighton Road, Croydon CR2 6EA; tel: 020 8760 5100, fax: 020 8760 0469, e-mail: expats@expat network.com, website: www.expatnetwork.co.uk;
- *Resident Abroad*, published by FT Finance, and available via the Subscriptions Department, PO Box 387, Haywards Heath, West Sussex RH16 3GS; tel: 01444 445520, fax: 01444 445599 (Europe, £59 plus VAT at local rates; rest of the world, £69).

In addition, Expat Network offers a total support service for expatriates. It is a leading expatriate membership organisation which enjoys a firmly established reputation within the overseas recruitment sector. The expatriate community and the overseas employment market need a level of understanding which can only be achieved over time. Most things are different, from the way in which contracts are negotiated, the job search itself, the problems involved with tax, personal finances, currency, locations, social security, pensions, etc. Expat Network can offer advice for each and every eventuality. A number of services are offered. The monthly magazine *Nexus* deals with expatriate issues, offers in-depth industry features, contractual news and has a 12-page job supplement. Some companies run their own; others use outside organisations. If your employer will not pay for you to attend a course, it would be worthwhile paying out of your own pocket. Ideally, both partners should attend, and children can also benefit.

Corona Worldwide runs one-day 'Living Overseas' briefings for men and women (price around £250) providing information and advice on living abroad and a one-to-one briefing, with a recent returner, on the country of your posting. Prices quoted are subject to revision. Emergency telephone and other briefings are also organised – fees for these can be obtained on request.

The Centre for International Briefing provides residential programmes and training for men and women taking up long-term appointments or short-term contracts abroad, and for home-based managers responsible for international personnel. Cultural and business briefings cover all major regions of the world, include all aspects of living and working, and allow a rapid transition to the destination country. Customised programmes provide training in international negotiation and communication skills, intercultural communication, international team-building and skill-transference in a foreign culture. Language tuition is also available, and the Centre's Language Plus programme combines intensive language and communication studies with business and cultural briefings. Details of programmes are available from the Customer Services Department, The Centre for International Briefing, Farnham Castle, Farnham GU9 0AG; tel: 01252 721194, fax: 01252 719277.

For expatriates going to Japan, China, Korea or other East Asian countries, individually prepared briefing and language sessions are available from East Asia Business Services at the University of Sheffield. Contact the EABS at 317 Glossop Road, Sheffield S10 2HP; tel: 0114 222 8060, fax: 0114 272 8028, e-mail: EABS@Sheffield.ac.uk. These briefings are tailor-made and can be residential or in-company, according to the client's requirements. Family participation is encouraged. Sister organisations in destinations can provide further services. Briefings are modular and designed to provide new skills and practical knowledge. Sessions are conducted by business people with specific experience of the region.

The External Services Division of the School of Oriental and African Studies within the University of London provides a wide range of briefing and language services for business/government and private individuals. Open briefings on Japan and China are offered on a regular basis, including the two-day Japan Business Orientation Programme and the China Business Orientation Programme. Briefings may be integrated with language tuition if required and are offered on a tailor-made basis for most of the countries or regions of Asia and Africa. Details are available from the Co-ordinator, Ms Dzidra Stipnieks, SOAS External Services Division, University of London, Thornhaugh Street, Russell Square, London WC1H 0XG; tel: 020 7898 4081.

Going Places Expatriate Briefing, 84 Coombe Road, New Malden, Surrey KT3 4QS; tel: 020 8949 8811, provide tailored briefings to individuals or groups, in-house or in the home. Briefings last from three hours to a full day and cover preparation, living in-country, working in-country, coming home. Expertise is available on over 50 countries for both the working and accompanying partner. Guideline costs indicate £950 plus VAT per day per individual or couple; £100 a head thereafter. Going Places will provide its own facilities if more convenient.

These courses, and some employers, arrange for you to meet recently returned expatriates, and this is particularly useful if you can work out in advance, preferably in the form of a checklist, what you and your family really need to know. Such a checklist can also be helpful if you are offered, as has become increasingly common for senior positions, the possibility of a 'look-see' visit to the location in question.

Some expatriates have reported that the British Council is often helpful in terms of overcoming entry shock and giving advice and information about local amenities and activities.

LEARNING A LANGUAGE

A further aspect of learning about the host country is to master a few basic greetings in the local language. Even when it is not strictly necessary, familiarity with the sound of a language makes everything seem less strange and it is appreciated locally.

The traditional picture of the Englishman who expects all foreigners to speak English or hopes to get by with schoolboy

French has disappeared. In the modern world of fast-moving communications, language proficiency is an essential tool. It is true that English is the world's leading language for business and commerce and, in non-English speaking countries, is taught in most schools as the second language. But in many countries knowledge of the indigenous language is essential and often a prerequisite of employment. It is vital where a job involves contact with local people, particularly in administration or industry, where orders and instructions have to be given and understood. Even where a job is technical and does not involve direct communication, it is an advantage to be able to join in conversation and be more fully integrated with local society.

Anybody working in the EU should be proficient in French and/or German. In Spain and Latin America, Spanish is essential (except in Brazil, where Portuguese is spoken). In the Third World, and in the Middle East, knowledge of indigenous languages is not so essential but it is useful to speak Arabic or Swahili, particularly in more remote areas. So the best thing you can do if you are going to work overseas is to learn one or more languages or brush up on your existing knowledge.

The increasing demand for languages is being met in a number of ways. There is the 'do-it-yourself' approach which can include:

1.   Learning at home, using Linguaphone courses or other self-study materials.
2.   Hiring a private tutor. Try to find a native speaker, who is prepared to conduct most of the lessons in the foreign language rather than waste valuable time talking about the language in English.
3.   Open learning courses at your local college of further education or university. Many have established 'drop in' centres where you have access to a language laboratory, and possibly also computer-assisted learning, with back-up from a tutor when you need it. This form of learning can be very effective for those whose time is limited and who need a flexible programme of study.

For those at the adult beginner level, *Oxford Beginner's Dictionaries*, published by Oxford University Press, offer all the words and phrases a beginner needs, as well as lots of extra help with learning including grammar, culture and travel information. *Beginner's Dictionaries* are available in French, German, Spanish, Italian, Russian, Chinese and

Japanese and are exceptionally easy to use because they move away from the traditional dictionary layout. All main translations are preceded by an equals sign so that they are instantly identifiable, and all parts of the entry are spelt out in full, avoiding confusing jargon and abbreviations. Grammar and usage notes throughout the text warn of possible translation pitfalls, and thousands of example phrases show how language is used in the context. The centre section of the dictionary gives background information on lifestyle and culture, tips on etiquette and interaction in the language, as well as a phrase finder, which provides useful travellers' phrases.

You may prefer to attend a language class, and these are run by most local authority adult education institutes and colleges. However, learning on the basis of one or two sessions a week is not the most effective way of getting to grips with a foreign language – you will make a lot more progress on a more intensive course.

Private language schools generally offer intensive or 'crash' courses. Be careful to check the bona fides of a course before you enrol. An example of the type of tuition available is Berlitz (UK) Ltd (9–13 Grosvenor Street, London W1A 3BZ; tel: 020 7915 0909, fax: 020 7915 0222), which offers language programmes to suit the linguistic needs for all in both the business and non-business fields. Berlitz offers crash courses, private lessons and semi-private courses for two to three people in most languages. The full-time Total Immersion® course lasts from one to six weeks for those wishing to improve their existing ability quickly. In-house courses for companies are also available.

Conrad Executive Language Training (15 King Street, London WC2E 8HN; tel: 020 7240 0855, fax: 020 7240 0715), founded in 1974, is specifically geared towards meeting the linguistic needs of business people. Tuition is structured to suit both the schedule of each client and specific language requirements. Classes can be held at Conrad's Covent Garden centre, in-company or privately, after a thorough language evaluation and needs analysis. Conrad is registered to ISO 9000 by BSI. Courses available: the Crash Course (9 am–4 pm), suitable for all levels and held over five days (not necessarily consecutively); and the Extensive Course, also suitable for all levels, which can be taken between 8 am and 8 pm – classes last at least one hour and are at times to suit the client. Conrad also offers cross-cultural training programmes for groups and individuals for all countries, and the Corporate Group Course (ideal for companies requiring language training for a small group of executives who have the same objectives and similar background knowledge).

The European Centre is a language consultancy helping individuals, companies and other organisations to communicate more effectively in international markets. Winner of two national awards in 1996, it specialises in the design, management and delivery of language training programmes for business and vocational purposes. All the programmes are designed to meet individual or corporate needs, based on a language assessment and training needs analysis. Further details from Jonathan Smith, The European Centre, Peter House, St Peter's Square, Manchester M1 5AN; tel: 0161 281 8844, fax: 0161 281 8822, e-mail: training@evcentre.co.uk.

Fees at language schools are high, but there is general agreement that they represent a worthwhile investment. Administrators of language schools sometimes complain that too few companies attach real importance to language proficiency and often leave it too late for effective action.

The Association of Language Excellence Centres (ALEC) is a professional body for providers of language training and related services for business. It aims to establish and maintain quality standards and help organisations and individuals to improve their performance in international markets, mergers and acquisitions with language training and consultancy geared to the needs of business, including: language training for business; translation and interpreting; country, cultural and trade briefings; needs analysis and language audits. For details of LX Centres in your area or application for membership contact Karen Wilkinson at ALEC, Cowley House, Little College Street, London SW1P 3XS; tel: 020 7222 0666, fax: 020 7233 0335, e-mail: kwilkinson@westminster.com.

Other options include foreign cultural institutes, such as the Alliance Française or the Goethe Institut, which run well-established courses, and organisations running courses abroad (nothing can beat learning a language in the country where it is spoken). Courses abroad are advertised in *The Times* and *The Guardian*.

Further information and advice are available from CILT (the Centre for Information on Language Teaching and Research), 20 Bedfordbury, London WC2N 4LB; tel: 020 7379 5101, fax: 020 7379 5082. Written enquiries are preferred. At the same address is NATBLIS, the National Business Language Information Service (tel: 020 7379 5131, fax: 020 7379 5082), which provides information on business language training and on providers of business language services – training, cultural briefing, interpreting and translation.

TAKE IT EASY

Once you arrive overseas you should take it easy, adjusting to climatic changes, as they will affect your physical and subsequently your mental state. Coping with so many new stimuli all at once is overpowering and you will need time to find your bearings. Tiredness and depression make it hard to react positively to your new situation. It is part of the adjustment cycle to feel frustrated and depressed, but if you can make the effort to understand the underlying cultural reasons for your frustration, you will be well on your way to adjusting successfully and enjoying your life abroad. After that you just have to cope with the culture shock of returning to the UK at the end of your assignment.

> ### Checklist: Adjusting to living and working abroad
>
> 1. Try to find out as much as possible about your host country – not just the physical conditions but its culture, values and beliefs.
> 2. Become familiar with the ground rules for behaviour towards colleagues and with attitudes to age and gender.
> 3. Be aware of the symptoms of stress and culture shock.
> 4. If you experience culture shock, find someone to talk to, perhaps an experienced expatriate, and seek professional help for prolonged symptoms.
> 5. Use the internet, public libraries and specialist services to find out as much information as possible about your new location.
> 6. Ask your employer to send you and your family on a briefing course before departure.
> 7. Try to learn the language of your host country – it will help you integrate into your local society.
> 8. Be aware that you might well experience culture shock on your return to your home country.

Part Four:

Making the Move

11 Moving Out

WHAT TO TAKE AND REMOVAL

Whatever agonising variables you feed into your mental computer about what and what not to take, you will certainly find that in the end you are left with two basic choices – either to take very little other than clothes, books, favourite possessions and whatever small items you and your family need to feel at home, or to take virtually everything.

It clearly depends on where you are going, how long you are going for, and who you are going to work for. If you are taking up an appointment in a sophisticated European capital or in North America, obviously you will not need the same kind of things as you would in a developing country, say in Africa or Asia, where everything tends to be scarce and expensive. If you are going to a tropical country, or the Middle East, clothes and equipment will be very different from what you will need in a temperate or northern area.

As a rule, travelling reasonably light is the best course of action. Even if you are going to be away for a long time, it seldom pays to take large items of household equipment, such as sofas, beds or wardrobes; the cost of shipping bulky items is very high. In any case, it can take quite a long time to clear them through customs when they arrive, so you will either have to send them ahead or find yourself arriving in a new place without any furniture.

Such situations are apt to be inconvenient and will probably result in your having to buy some things simply to tide you over. Clothes, bedlinen, crockery, kitchen equipment and so forth are cheap to transport – shipping companies usually convey some baggage free of charge – and usually expensive to replace at the other end. Furthermore, these items lend themselves to being sent ahead, and you can usually make do, or borrow, in the meantime.

Antiques are always worth taking, since they are vastly expensive in most places outside the UK, but remember that old furniture and pictures can be sensitive to climatic change. Such problems may also exist with electronic equipment, and your CD player or food mixer may have to go through costly adaptations to fit in with foreign voltages. Records, tapes and musical instruments deteriorate in hot climates. There can also be problems over import controls, though most authorities have special dispensations for personal possessions.

As far as household equipment is concerned, much depends on the terms of your contract. Most commercial firms in developing countries will provide a fully furnished house or apartment (possibly also a car). Fully furnished means that everything, down to the last lampshade, is provided and you only need your personal effects. National governments and public corporations usually supply 'hard furnished' accommodation. Hard furnished is what it implies. Only the bare necessities such as tables and chairs and a bed are provided, and you will need to supply curtains, cushions, linen, loose covers, cutlery, crockery and kitchen gear. Often you can buy these things from an outgoing tenant or returning expatriate, but you have to be on the spot for this.

It is strongly recommended that where a family is going out to a developing country the employee should travel out alone in advance, unless furnished accommodation is assured, and only send for the family when this has been fixed up. It may mean staying in a hotel or hostel for a time, but it is worth the inconvenience to be able to learn the ropes at first hand and decide what will be needed from home. Some companies arrange for both partners to go out in advance for a 'reconnaissance' visit.

In some cases, especially if the contract is a short-term one, in a difficult country, it is recommended that the employee should go out alone, leaving his or her family in the UK. This may sound heartless, but it does minimise the upheaval and avoids disrupting the children's education.

If you are going to a tropical country where conditions are difficult, you may not be able to buy such items as a deep freeze, food mixer, sewing machine, hairdryer and electric iron except in the main centres. A portable electric fan is useful if the house is not air conditioned. An electric kettle is a must and so is a torch. There may be power cuts, so stock up with candles.

If you have very young children with you, take pram, carrycot, pushchair and plenty of toys. Camping equipment, eg tents and sleeping bags, may be useful, and so may gardening tools, as many houses have quite large gardens. Take golf clubs, tennis rackets, photographic equipment, etc, since these leisure and luxury goods may be unobtainable or very expensive overseas, though this will again depend very much on where you go.

Stock up with cosmetics and toiletries, drugs and medicines since everything in this line is expensive and difficult to obtain. Find out the voltage and type of electric plug in use and, before you go if possible, check with the appliance manufacturer about any adaptations. A useful website address is www.kropla.com which is a comprehensive listing of worldwide electrical and telephone information and provides details of electric plugs and voltages used in different countries throughout the world.

Don't rely on somebody sending you something from home. Postage can be exorbitant, mails are slow and the contents liable to be pilfered. It may be possible to get your children, or your neighbour's children, to bring things out when they come on leave from school.

The best way to handle the question of actual removal is to consult one of the big removal firms. Overseas removal is not a job you should take on yourself, nor is it a good thing on which to try to save money. Moving abroad is a very different proposition from moving in this country and, in choosing your remover, it is better to ask for a good name than a good quote. The bigger removers are well informed about living conditions in overseas countries – check, though, that any printed literature they give you is fully up to date.

Removers are knowledgeable about what you can and should take with you, and most have agents at ports of entry who can help with the sometimes interminable business of clearing your belongings through customs. Another advantage of a 'name' remover is that they can generally get a better insurance deal than with a smaller firm. You should, incidentally, increase your insurance to cover replacement costs at the other end. If you cannot get any specific information about this, an increase of 50 to 80 per cent over UK values will serve as a rough guideline.

An alternative to using one of the 'big names' is to contact one of the specialist consortia of overseas removal companies. These are made up of hand-picked, privately owned companies specialising in overseas removals. As a team, members provide the strength and capacity of a large international concern; individually they are able to provide a local, personal service that many customers prefer.

All members conform to standards of service that are the same all over the world. So a remover operating out of the UK will provide the same level of service as his or her counterparts in Italy, for instance. Using the consortium method is rather like using a removal company with branch offices all over the world.

In the past there has been extensive publicity over the sudden demise of overseas removal companies, which – having received payment in advance – have left their customers' belongings either in the warehouse or, worse still, languishing in an overseas country. This usually resulted in families having to pay twice over for their household effects to be delivered, and many who could not afford to pay again had to abandon their belongings altogether.

Protection against this sort of disaster is now available through the Advance Payments Guarantee Scheme operated by the Overseas Group of the British Association of Removers. The Scheme provides that customers who have paid removal charges in advance to a firm participating in the Scheme are guaranteed that, in the event of the removal company ceasing to trade, their belongings will either be delivered at no further cost, or they will be refunded the cost of the removal charges.

It should not be assumed that all removers are in the Scheme. The safeguard provided by the Scheme is available only through members of the BAR Overseas Group. The guarantee is underwritten by a mutual insurance company set up by the industry.

The British Association of Removers itself will be happy to supply readers with leaflets giving advice on moving abroad and brochures on the Advance Payments Guarantee Scheme. The Association also provides a list of companies participating in the Scheme. Readers should send a 9in × 4in sae to the British Association of Removers, 3 Churchill Court, 58 Station Road, North Harrow HA2 7SA (tel: 020 8861 3331, fax: 020 8861 3332).

Removal costs vary according to the distance to be covered, the method of transportation (land, sea or air), the terms of the arrangement (delivery to port or home, packed or unpacked) and a range of other factors. Customers should obtain *written* estimates from several companies. Beware of firms that quote on the basis of approximate measures. Be specific, understand exactly the terms of the arrangement and obtain a written agreement, so that you have what amounts to a contract with which to resist 'surcharges' imposed at the point of disembarkation.

Some people like to pack their own things. If so, it is best to use custom-made cardboard boxes, which are stout, light and can be banded to withstand rough handling and exposure. These generally come with movers' details, logo and grids in which details of the contents, origin and whether fragile or not, can be entered. It is essential to make a list of contents and advisable to see that your cases or boxes are readily identifiable for when you collect them at the other end. Smaller goods can be taken with you, up to the 20 kg allowable limit. Some things may be carried as hand luggage, depending on how full the plane is. But on all these points, be guided by the experts.

MOVING SMOOTHLY TO A NEW WORKING LIFE

Philip Pertoldi, Managing Director of Abels Moving Services, offers guidance on what needs to be considered in planning a move to make it as painless as possible.

Moving home can be one of life's most stressful events. Effective planning is the key to making it as smooth as possible. Whether the move is being organised by a company or an individual, an understanding of what is involved will help achieve the best outcome.

What needs to be considered is the selecting of an international relocation company and the moving process from the initial survey through to packing, shipping, storage and insurance. A removals supplier can provide a personal assistant to facilitate a comprehensive relocation service to alleviate most of the stress of a move, especially for the accompanying family.

What should you look for in would-be suppliers? There are a number of quality standards to check when making selections. First, there is ISO 9001:2000, an international standard awarded to companies that is only achieved after a thorough audit of their procedures against tough criteria and that indicates a professionally run organisation. Secondly, there is a FAIM accreditation, which is a quality standard set by FIDI, the only worldwide organisation of note for the industry. Thirdly, in the UK, only a company regulated by the Financial Services Authority (FSA) can offer insurance products. Finally, all will claim they have trained staff, but select those that have met the Investor in People standard.

Organising a survey at your home allows you to meet the company's representative, to show him or her what needs to be moved and to have a discussion on the service that best meets your requirements. The representative should be knowledgeable and be able to answer then or later all your concerns. For the company, the representative can assess what resources will be appropriate to fulfil the contract in a safe and secure manner.

The condition of your treasured belongings when they arrive at your new home will largely depend upon the way they were packed: specifically, the skills of the packing crew and the quality of packing materials. Generally, it is best left to the experts, as different levels of packing are needed for different forms of transportation. Another reason is the heightened security at customs points around the world, where customs officials now will insist on checking owner-packed goods, causing delays and potential damage.

Concerning shipping, large-move volumes can be shipped in their own exclusive container. There are three sizes of container: 20 feet, 40 feet and lastly to some locations 45 feet. Unless the goods are stored beforehand, the container will be packed and sealed at the property that is being moved out of, and then the goods will be shipped on the next available vessel to the necessary port of entry overseas. Consignments too small to fill a container, called less than a container load (LCL), can be individually overcased and then loaded into a shipping container at port, and shipped reasonably quickly.

A more economic way, but potentially needing a longer period of time, is groupage. Here, the goods are packed in the home and then returned to the mover's warehouse to be consolidated with other customer loads, which are then secured into a shipping container prior to being despatched to the port for shipment.

In the case of rapid transit being required, the goods can be despatched by airfreight, where they are packed into palletised modules ready for immediate transportation. This is often used for small consignments or essential items needed for early use.

Moves to mainland Europe are completed by road transportation, when the move is either in an appropriate-sized pantechnicon or as a part-load with other consignments on the same vehicle sharing the costs. Again transit time requirements will influence the mode and expense.

It is not unusual for an international move at one point or another to involve storage. For example, long-term storage may be required when someone lets out his or her home while being posted abroad to furnished rented accommodation, or short-term storage may be needed in the UK or overseas because of a new home not being ready on time. It is advisable to check for secure and well-maintained premises where the items will be stored.

Specialist movers should offer all risk insurance regulated by the FSA, which covers goods while in transit, during incidental storage en route and while professionally stored. It is usually available at an additional cost. There are many factors to consider in selecting the most appropriate insurance, which include the level of cover, whether the policy offers 'like for like' (reinstatement) or 'new for old' (replacement), the exclusions and the excess.

Insurance is complicated, but it is essential customers understand the nature and level of the cover they are taking out. They should ensure that a summary of the cover document is supplied by the remover and that it states all the necessary information and makes clear what has to be done for them to be insured correctly.

It is crucial to consider insurance at the start of planning a move. For many, the worry that their treasured items may be damaged or lost during the move is lifted by the assumption that they are fully insured. However, this may not always be the case.

As discussed, relocating overseas can be complex, involving planning and meticulous attention to detail. Recognising this, some removal companies have broadened their services and include full move management, that is, the complete organisation of much more than just the moving of the household effects.

The person who is moving because of work often has little choice in the area he or she relocates to. The culture can be completely unknown, the language different and the bureaucratic system incomprehensible. Time is often restricted on such moves, with little allowance made for transition. In such cases it is essential to find a company that can work either with the individual or with the individual's company to ensure the relocation as a whole is as smooth and as uncomplicated as possible. By using a company that provides orientation services and puts itself in charge of all the necessary research, the whole situation can be made much easier.

Abels International Services can offer a full relocation package. Not only will Abels plan the move but it will also provide an overview of the area the client wishes to move to. Should clients wish, they can ask for an orientation of the chosen area where they will be accompanied on a tour of the location with emphasis on aspects such as housing, transportation, education, health care, banking and finance, and leisure. Abels will also compile an information pack with useful websites and information to help the transition phase and especially to help the partner and family.

There is definitely a need for the complete service in relocating overseas. The sheer scale of the task and the amount of time usually allocated to it mean that more and more individuals are leaving it to the professionals to shoulder the burden and provide that extra touch to ensure as stress-free a move as possible. Don't you deserve the same?

PETS

Pets often pose a problem. Some shipping companies and airlines require a bill of health from a veterinary surgeon. In all cases, before leaving the UK you should first obtain an export health certificate from the Department for Environment, Food and Rural Affairs (DEFRA). There are a number of specialist animal shipping services available. You will need to apply in good time beforehand to DEFRA for an information pack so that you can make the necessary arrangements. Quarantine has been replaced by a vaccination and electronic tagging procedure for animals being transported to and from rabies-free and EU countries. Details can be found on the DEFRA website www.defra.gov.uk.

Checklist: Choice of removers

1. The remover should provide a free estimate and a written quote.
2. Does the quote specify *professional* packing under your general supervision?
3. How will fragile items, furniture and articles be packed?
4. What insurance cover is offered? If there is any excess (ie a minimum figure below which you will not be reimbursed), what is it?
5. Can the removers immediately provide the name and address of the port agents at your destination?
6. Will they deliver to your residence at the other end, or will you have to arrange clearance yourself? Check that the quotation specifies whether the goods will be delivered to residence or to port only.
7. What proportion of their current business is in overseas removals?

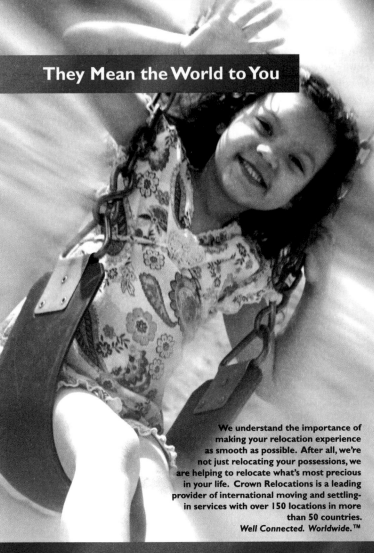

They Mean the World to You

We understand the importance of making your relocation experience as smooth as possible. After all, we're not just relocating your possessions, we are helping to relocate what's most precious in your life. Crown Relocations is a leading provider of international moving and settling-in services with over 150 locations in more than 50 countries.
Well Connected. Worldwide.™

Household shipments • Storage • Children's programmes
Online tracking • Insurance • Immigration assistance
Home & school search • Intercultural training

Call us at 0800 919940
email us at enquiries.uk@crownrelo.com
or visit **www.moveoverseas.co.uk**

CROWN
R E L O C A T I O N S

VAT

You will almost certainly find that some of the things you want are cheaper to buy here, even allowing for shipping charges. You should make sure that you take full advantage of the various VAT export schemes under which a UK resident going abroad can escape having to pay UK VAT altogether. There are two schemes, one for motor vehicles and one for other goods.

Motor vehicles

If you will be living outside the EU

You have to purchase your new vehicle from a dealer who operates the Personal Export Scheme. He or she will give you VAT Form 410 to fill in, which will require you to fulfil certain conditions. The relevant notes are found in VAT Notice 705. Motor cycles and motor caravans are also covered by this scheme.

■ You must personally take delivery of the vehicle, and it must be used only by you, or someone else who is also leaving the EU and has your permission to use it.

■ You have to take the vehicle abroad within 6 months of delivery, or within 12 months if you have lived outside the EU for more than 365 days in the previous two years, or more than 1,095 days in the previous six years.

■ You and the car must remain outside the EU for at least six consecutive months.

Alternatively, the supplier can deliver the car directly to your destination, free of VAT. See VAT Notice 703.

If you will be living within the EU

You must complete Form VAT 411, supplied by the motor dealer.

■ The vehicle must be new, and you must take it to your destination within two months of delivery. Cars must not have been driven for more than 1,864 miles in this time.

■ You must declare the vehicle to the member state's fiscal authority.

After you have had the vehicle abroad for at least 12 months you may re-import it without paying VAT, provided you are either a diplomat, a member of an officially recognised international organisation, a member of NATO or returning UK Forces personnel or you can prove that the duty and tax have been paid. Otherwise you will have to pay VAT on the value of the vehicle at the time of re-importation. If you return to the UK within six months of the date of export, the full amount of VAT on the sale must be paid. If the vehicle is found to be in the UK after the date for its export shown on the registration document (ie six months from purchase date if you are leaving the EU, or two months otherwise), you will have to pay VAT in full and it will also be liable to forfeiture. This applies even if failure to export the vehicle is due to circumstances beyond your control (eg theft or destruction). Therefore, while the car is still in the UK, before export, it is essential to insure it for its full value, including potential VAT. Obviously, it is important to license, register and insure the vehicle if you will be using it in the UK before departure.

Other goods

If you have been in the EU for more than 365 days in the previous two years and are going to a final destination outside the EU for at least 12 consecutive months, you may buy goods using the Retail Export Scheme. At participating retailers, you must ask to complete VAT Form 435 at the time of purchase. To receive a refund equal to the amount of VAT you must get this form certified by a customs authority when the goods are exported – the goods must be delivered to your shipper or freight forwarder at your final point of departure from the EU. You cannot take delivery of them in this country. The refund is then paid by the retailer, not HM Revenue and Customs (HMRC). See VAT Notices 704 and 704/1. As there is a lot of documentation involved, you may find this procedure is not worth your while unless you are making fairly large purchases and only in one or two shops.

TAKING A CAR ABROAD

British people tend to prefer right-hand drive and will therefore consider buying their car here and taking it with them. First check at the embassy of the country you propose to live in that private car imports are permitted.

Probably the best way to plan this is to make a list of what you will want your car to do. The road surfaces may be worse than those you are used to, so you may consider taking a good second-hand car rather than a brand new one. You will not then be so worried about driving through very narrow streets. In some places drivers actually park by shunting the cars ahead and behind!

If you buy a new car in the UK before going abroad, you can use it here for six months, run it in and have your first service before you take it overseas. Check the servicing facilities in the area where you plan to live. It would be unwise to take a car abroad if the nearest dealer service is 70 miles away. This factor may well limit your choice.

A big car will be expensive with petrol and difficult to park. If you will be living in an apartment and there is no garage, the car will usually be left in the street and possibly for long periods at that. Consider carefully the security of your car and what you may have in it. Choose a model with locking wheel nuts and high-quality locks so that it is hard to get into without smashing the windows. Radio thefts are prevalent in some countries; therefore you may wish to consider a demountable radio.

Should you decide to take a small car to a hot country, always buy one with a sun roof because the smaller cars tend not to carry air conditioning.

People moving to Spain will often choose diesel cars because the fuel is half the price of petrol and easily available. Lead-free petrol is now available in many countries and you should check whether your engine will take this quality. Some engines need minor adaptation.

The other possibility is to hire a car in the UK. First check whether the hire company is happy with your destination and route. Restrictions depend on insurance cover for more out-of-the-way locations. You should also have the hirer provide you with proof of ownership – in this case form VE103a. Hirers are more than happy to do business with expatriates because of the length of hire and the fact that most are credit- and trustworthy. With regard to this latter point, it will be essential to pay by credit card.

Taking your existing car abroad

If you take the car you own at present abroad for longer than 12 months, this is regarded as a permanent export and the procedure is described in leaflet V526, obtainable from your local Vehicle Registration Office.

The following procedure applies to exports from England, Scotland, Wales and the Isles of Scilly only, not to Northern Ireland, the Isle of Man or the Channel Islands, where cars are registered separately.

Complete section 2 on the back of the Vehicle Registration Document, entering the proposed date of export, and send the document to your local Vehicle Registration Office or to the Driver and Vehicle Licensing Centre. This should be done well in advance of your departure.

You will receive back a Certificate of Export (V561) which in effect confirms your vehicle registration and replaces the vehicle registration document (V5). Some countries, however, are failing to recognise this certificate as a registration document, which can cause problems when you wish to re-register your vehicle in another country.

A different procedure applies in Northern Ireland, the Isle of Man and the Channel Islands, where vehicles are registered locally; it is necessary to register and license a car taken *to* these places for over 12 months as soon as the current British tax disc expires, if not before. The Certificate of Export mentioned above will still be necessary, although these authorities may accept the vehicle registration document for re-registration purposes.

Motoring services in Europe

The Alliance Internationale de Tourisme (AIT) has its headquarters in Geneva, and motoring clubs throughout Europe are affiliated to it, including the Royal Automobile Club and the Automobile Association. There is also the Federation Internationale de l'Automobile, based in Paris, of which the RAC is a member. These clubs provide a wide range of services to each other's members travelling abroad, so membership of one is worthwhile.

CUSTOMS

Regulations and procedures vary. Most customs authorities allow you to take in used things for your personal use and often let people, eg newly married couples, bring in new things duty free. Wherever possible keep receipts to show to the customs officials.

In most places, you are allowed to take in 'household and used personal effects', including refrigerators, radios, TV receivers and minor electrical appliances, but duties on new items of this kind are usually fairly steep. There are bans everywhere on guns, plants and drugs. Many Middle East and North African countries operate a boycott list, so do not take anything without checking the situation. Duty free wines, spirits and tobacco up to a certain amount – check with the airline – are normally allowed, except in most Middle East countries.

ESSENTIALS BEFORE YOU GO

There are certain things you must see about before you actually leave. There are obvious chores, like cancelling milk and papers, etc. Have a thorough medical check for yourself and your family before you go, including teeth and eyes. Some jobs, of course, depend on physical fitness. Make sure you have the necessary vaccination certificates and check the requirements. Most tropical countries need certificates against smallpox and possibly cholera and yellow fever; other vaccinations may be advisable. If you are going to the tropics you should contact your GP about anti-malarial precautions. For the most up-to-date advice on malaria in the region where you are going, you should contact the Malaria Reference Laboratory at the London School of Hygiene and Tropical Medicine.

In many countries it is advisable to include a rabies injection in your schedule of jabs for yourself and members of your family. You should also warn children of the perils of cuddling strange animals which may harbour other diseases in addition to the rabies threat.

Check that you have all your documents to hand – up-to-date passport, visas, cheque book, permits, health certificates, letter of appointment. Take spare passport photos – it is probably best for partners to have separate passports – and all your diplomas and references, even birth and marriage certificates. The appetite for documents is well-nigh insatiable in some countries!

Melancholy though it may sound, you should also make some provision for the unthinkable: instructions in the case of death, disablement or catastrophe while you are abroad. Contact your financial adviser or insurance company for more information.

If you have a reliable solicitor, you might also consider the possibility of giving him or her power of attorney. This is a simple legal transaction that essentially means that the person having that power can act in your stead. If you need a large sum of money to be sent out to you in a hurry, it is very useful to have a responsible person in the UK whom you can fax and who can raise the money from your bank. Likewise, if you have left your house in the hands of managing agents who are not doing their stuff, you need someone on the spot who can sort things out. Giving someone power of attorney obviously implies a high degree of trust, but there are occasions when it could save you the cost of a return fare home.

KEEPING YOUR VOTE WHILE LIVING ABROAD

On moving abroad, you retain your right to vote in UK and European parliamentary elections; however, there are a number of conditions of which you should be aware. To be eligible you must be a British citizen and satisfy *either* of two sets of conditions:

Set 1

- you have previously been on the electoral register for an address in the UK;
- you were living there on the qualifying date;*
- there are no more than 20 years between the qualifying dates for that register and the one on which you now wish to appear.

Set 2

- you last lived in the UK less than 20 years before the qualifying date for the register on which you wish to appear;
- you were too young to be on the electoral register, which was based on the last qualifying date before you left;
- a parent or guardian was on the electoral register for the address where you were living on that date;
- you are at least 18 years old, or will become 18 when the register comes into force.

---

*The qualifying date in England, Scotland and Wales is 10 October each year and in Northern Ireland, 15 September. This is for the electoral register, which comes into force on 16 February of the following year and remains in force for 12 months from that date.

You have to register every year on or before the qualifying date and you may continue to register while overseas for 20 years from the qualifying date for the last electoral register on which you appeared as a UK resident.

How to register

To register you must fill in an Overseas Elector's Declaration form RPF 37, which you can get from the nearest British consular or diplomatic mission. The following information will be required: your full name and overseas address, the UK address where you were last registered and the date you left the UK. The first-time overseas elector will have to find someone to support the declaration who is aged 18 or over, has a British passport and is a British citizen, is not living in the UK and who knows you but is not a close relative. First-time overseas electors who left the UK before they were old enough to register will also have to provide a copy of their full birth certificate and information about the parent or guardian on whose registration they are relying.

How to vote and remain registered

You do not have a postal vote. Instead you must appoint a proxy who will vote on your behalf. He or she must be a citizen of Britain, the Commonwealth or the Republic of Ireland, a UK resident, and willing and legally able to vote on your behalf. The application form for appointing a proxy is attached to the Overseas Elector's Declaration form. Your declaration, proxy application and, if required, birth certificate should be returned to the electoral registration officer for the area where you were last registered. The electoral registration officer will write to tell you whether you qualify as an overseas elector and will be included on the register: if you do not, he or she will explain why. You will be sent a reminder each year, and another declaration form will be enclosed with this.

REMOVAL NOTIFICATIONS

Don't forget to tell the following organisations that you are moving abroad:

Your bank.

Income Tax Office. Notify HMRC giving the exact date of departure.

Contributions Agency, International Services (for information on National Insurance contributions and related health cover), Longbenton, Newcastle upon Tyne, NE98 1YX, or *The Benefits Agency, Pensions and Overseas Benefits Directorate* (for advice on benefits and related health cover), at Tyneview Park, Newcastle upon Tyne NE98 1BA. Include your full name, date of birth and UK NI or pension number, together with details of the country to which you are moving and the duration of your stay.

Vehicle licence. If you are taking your vehicle abroad for longer than a year this is regarded as a 'permanent export'. In this case you should return your existing (new-style) registration document to the Driver and Vehicle Licensing Centre, Swansea SA99 1AB, filling in the 'permanent export' section. Alternatively, you can apply to your local Vehicle Registration Office for the necessary forms.

Driving licence. You will probably want to retain your British driving licence. Some countries recognise it as valid and a list of those that do not is available from the RAC and the AA.

International Driving Permit. An International Driving Permit is obtainable from the RAC or AA (even if you are not a member) and is valid for one year. The licence is not valid in the country where it is issued so you must obtain it before leaving the UK. Most countries require residents to hold a local driving licence so check whether this is the case on taking up your new residence. Contact RAC Travel Services, PO Box 1500, Bristol BS99 2LH (telephone 0800 550055 for information), or any Automobile Association shop.

Motor insurance. Notify your insurers of the date of your departure – your insurance should be cancelled from that date and you should obtain a refund for the rest of the insurance period. Ask your insurance company for a letter outlining your no-claims record to show to your new insurer.

Life and other insurances. Notify the companies concerned or your insurance broker if you use one.

Council tax. Notify the town hall.

Dentist and optician. Let them know you are moving, as a matter of courtesy. It will save posting useless check-up reminders.

Private health insurance. Notify subscriber records department.

Gas. If you use it, notify your local gas supplier giving at least *48 hours'* notice. They will give you a standard form to fill in with details of the move and any current hire-purchase agreements. If appliances are to be removed they require as much notice as possible to arrange an appointment; there is a disconnection charge.

Electricity. Notify your local district office or showroom at least *48 hours* before moving. Arrangements are much the same as for gas.

Water. The local water board should also be notified at least *48 hours* before the move. Drain tanks and pipes if the house is to remain empty in winter.

Telephone. Notify your local telephone sales office as shown in the front of your directory at least *seven days* before the move.

Libraries. Return books and give in tickets to be cancelled.

Professional advisers such as solicitors, accountants, stockbrokers, insurance brokers, etc. Make sure they have a forwarding address.

Stocks and shares. Write to the company registrar at the address on the last annual report or share certificates.

Organisations and clubs – any business, civic, social, cultural, sports or automobile club of which you are a member. For the AA write to Membership Subscriptions and Records, PO Box 50, Basingstoke, Hampshire RG21 2ED and for the RAC write to Membership Enquiries, PO Box 1500, Bristol BS99 2LH.

Credit card companies. Advise them that you are leaving the country.

Hire purchase and rental companies. Notify the office where repayments are made. You will need to settle your account.

Local business accounts – department stores, newsagents, dairy, baker, chemist, dry cleaner, laundry, motor service station.

Publications. Cancel postal subscriptions to newspapers, magazines, professional and trade journals, book and record clubs, etc.

National Health Service. Return your NHS card to the Family Health Services Authority for your area, giving your date of departure, or hand it in to the immigration officer at your point of departure.

Pension schemes. If you have a 'frozen' or paid-up pension from a previous employer notify the pension trust of your new address.

TV. If you have a rented set, make arrangements to return it.

Post Office. Notify day of departure and UK contact address.

Personal Giro. The Post Office has a special sae for this.

Premium Bonds – anything rather than join the sad list of unclaimed prizes! Contact Premium Bonds, National Savings, Blackpool FY3 9XR to check the current position, because in a few countries, Premium Bond holdings may contravene lottery laws.

Save As You Earn and National Savings Certificates. It is important to notify any permanent change of address. Advise the Savings and Certificates and SAYE Office, Durham DH99 1NS, quoting the contract number(s).

National Savings Bank. Notify at Glasgow G58 1SB.

National Savings Income Bonds. Notify Income Bonds, Blackpool FY3 9YP.

Your landlord. If you are a tenant, give the appropriate notice to quit.

Your tenants. If you are a landlord, that UK address you've organised will be needed.

Your employer. Give new address details, or a contact address, in writing.

Schools. Try to give your children's schools a term's notice that they will be leaving. If you wish your children's education to be continued in Britain, contact your local education authority or the Department for Education and Employment, Sanctuary Buildings, Great Smith Street, London SW1P 3BT, for advice, and see Chapter 8.

Make sure your *removers* have any temporary contact address and phone numbers for you, both in the UK and abroad, so that they can get in touch with you when the need arises. It is also useful for them if you can tell them when you expect to arrive in your new country.

Checklist: Moving out

1. Be practical about what to take and try to travel light.
2. Check what will be available in your new accommodation and consider whether it might be better for the working partner to go out ahead of the rest of the family.
3. Consult with a reputable removal firm with experience in overseas removal.
4. Increase your insurance to cover replacement costs at the other end.
5. If you have a pet, think about what will be the best arrangement in the long term. If you are taking your dog with you, be sure to arrange for vaccination six months before you leave.
6. Think carefully about whether or not you should take your car with you, as it might not be suitable for the terrain of your new home.
7. If you decide to take your car, obtain leaflet V562 from your local Vehicle Registration Office.
8. Have a thorough medical check-up before you leave.
9. Check that you have all your documents available and take spare passport photos.
10. Fill in an Overseas Elector's Declaration form RPF37 to keep your right to vote.

$\boxed{12}$ Settling In

You arrive, with or without your family, and may find you are not met at the airport. This is the first of many irritations which people going out to work for overseas governments may encounter. It does not usually happen with companies. You may have to stay in a hotel or hostel for a considerable time, so make sure in advance who is going to foot the bill. You will need money to meet such contingencies – and to pay for telephones and taxis to and from the airport.

Even if you are lucky enough to move into a house or apartment, you will find a bare larder. This is where any tins or packet foods you brought with you will come in useful. (In Jamaica, the Corona Worldwide branch will provide a loan of a 'basket' of essentials for people waiting for their baggage to be unloaded.)

One early need will be to fix up domestic help, if you want it. It is usually best to engage a house steward and/or any other servants on the personal recommendation of the previous occupant (you may inherit his or her staff) or a neighbour. Find out from the local labour office what the going rate is and negotiate accordingly, making it quite clear from the start what duties the staff will be expected to perform, eg in the kitchen, washing and housework. Living quarters are usually provided, but find out beforehand whether your steward plans to bring all his family and relatives to stay with him!

Both for insurance purposes and your own peace of mind, make proper security arrangements. Some people, either individually or in groups, employ nightwatchmen; others rely on dogs, or on special locks. The extent of pilfering and burglary in many African countries has grown alarmingly in recent years, so make sure your precautions are fully adequate. John Wason (Insurance Brokers)

Ltd, founded by a former expatriate, offers a specialist Overseas Personal Insurance scheme, which includes home contents, belongings, money and personal liability, as well as optional medical and accident/sickness cover. It is claimed to be the only such policy available on a stand-alone basis, and as such would be useful for those in rented or company property.

At an early stage it is a good idea to see to all your requirements for banking and for obtaining work and residence permits, income tax coding, and the driving licence and test requirements where necessary. Find out also about health products and medical facilities, contributions to provident funds and subscriptions to clubs. Many employers pay for these.

Finally, keep a close eye on the health of young children, particularly on persistent tummy upsets and fevers. It is advisable always to use water you have sterilised yourself, not bottled water of unknown provenance.

There is also the question of preparation, other than physical, for your move. Do you know what the country you are going to is like? What facilities are there for shopping, leisure and entertainment? What is the climate like and what clothes will you need? Are there any pitfalls you should know about or any special behavioural dos and don'ts? Nowadays, overseas countries are very sensitive about foreigners understanding that their new patterns of government and economic development are not just pale imitations of the West.

The importance of getting properly briefed beforehand cannot be overestimated. This will not only save you from possible embarrassing situations – for example, if you don't know the rules about drinking in the Middle East – but will help you to decide what you need to take with you and give you some idea of the atmosphere in which you will work and live. Companies specialising in country-specific briefings are described in Chapter 10. Details can also be found in the website directory at the back of this book.

GOING THROUGH DIPLOMATIC CHANNELS

Expatriates who work for British companies or those from other Western countries in the developing or newly industrialised world can usually expect their employers to come to their aid in case of a political upheaval, or even if they get into personal difficulties – deserved or otherwise. Furthermore, they can expect their contracts of employment to be clear-cut and to conform to Western norms. Neither of these things is necessarily true if you work for a local employer, as is increasingly the case. The money is often better, but the risk is greater.

Some guidance on points to watch out for in taking up an appointment with a local employer in a developing country is given in the Employment Conditions Checklist in Chapter 2. Ultimately, though, you have no protection other than your own vigilance and UK diplomatic channels in the country concerned. They are generally very much criticised by expatriates as being ineffectual or indifferent, but the Foreign and Commonwealth Office claim this is because their role is not understood. For a start, they cannot intervene in contractual disputes, *unless* a British subject is being discriminated against in comparison with other employees. They can, however, recommend you a local lawyer who may be able to help you and they maintain carefully vetted lists of reliable legal firms. Best of all, they say, is to write to the British embassy or consulate nearest to your location before you leave the UK and ask them to put you in touch with someone who can give you a line on your prospective employer. Though UK diplomatic sources do keep track of known bad hats among employers, in the main they prefer such information to go through non-diplomatic channels, for obvious reasons.

The consular service of the Foreign Office is now very sensitive about the criticisms that have been made of it. If you fail to get an answer from the embassy or consulate you have contacted, or you are not satisfied with the service provided at a British embassy, high commission or consulate, you should write to: Director of Consular Services, Consular Directorate, Foreign & Commonwealth Office, Old Admiralty Building, Whitehall, London SW1A 2PA; tel: 020 7008 0223, fax: 020 7008 0152.

Primarily, of course, the role of British diplomats is to protect British subjects from the consequences of political upheavals. Any expatriate who goes to a notoriously high-risk place must take into account the circumstances there before deciding to accept an appointment. Diplomats are also not able to protect you from the consequences if you break the law of the land you are in. At most they can visit you in prison, arrange for you to be properly repre-sented legally and intercede discreetly for an amnesty for you. A

UK or multinational company would, in such cases, arrange for you to be flown out on the first available plane, usually with the connivance of the authorities.

Whatever your feelings about the efficacy or otherwise of British diplomatic protection, you should register with the embassy or consulate as soon as possible after you arrive to work in any developing country. This means they can contact you if a sudden emergency arises, whether personal or political. It cannot do any harm; and if you wake up one morning to the sound of gunfire, as has happened to many an expatriate, you may be very glad that you took that precaution.

Foreign & Commonwealth Travel Advice is designed to help British travellers avoid trouble by providing succinct and up-to-date information on threats to personal safety arising from political unrest, lawlessness, violence, natural disasters and epidemics. Some 650 notices are issued each year covering more than 130 countries. Notices are constantly renewed on the basis of information from posts overseas. The full range of notices is available on BBC2 Ceefax pages 470 onwards, and on the FCO's website, along with a range of Consular Division publicity material, www.fco.gov.uk. The public can contact the Travel Advice Unit direct between 9.30 am and 4.00 pm Monday to Friday on 0870 606 0290.

Other Consular Services information leaflets, including *Checklist for Travellers*, *Backpackers and Independent Travellers* and *British Consular Services Abroad* are widely distributed through travel agents, shipping companies and airlines, public libraries, Citizens Advice Bureaux and the UK Passport Agency, and can be obtained by faxing the Distribution Centre on 01444 246620.

READING MATTER

You may never have been much of a book buyer while living in the UK, but many expatriates report that not being able to get hold of books when they want them is an unexpected deprivation, especially in postings where other forms of entertainment, at any rate in English, are hard to come by.

Many places do, of course, have bookshops which stock some English titles, but the selection is often very limited (children's books are particularly hard to get) and prices are always much higher than the UK price shown tantalisingly on the jacket. You can, however, import your own books at standard London prices through the admirable Good Book Guide (23 Bedford Avenue, London WC1B 3AX; 24-hour tel: 020 7323 3636 (UK), +44 (0)20 7323 3838 (from outside UK), e-mail: enquiries@gbgdirect.com) or order books on the internet from Amazon.com. The Guide is a mail order book service with a substantial trade among expatriates all over the world. You can choose your books from the monthly guide, for which there is a modest annual subscription, but the service can also get any book in print for you, including paperbacks. There are also regular video and audio listings offering a wealth of entertainment: drama, documentary, comedy and children's programmes.

The choices in the guide are accompanied by brief, helpful notes written by outside experts (eg Chris Bonington on travel) and the selection of titles is broad, covering both high-brow literature and commercial best sellers, all chosen on merit alone. The subject areas are broad too, ranging through all kinds of interests. However, the Good Book Guide is not a book club – there is no obligation to buy. A free trial issue can be requested.

Payment is on a cash with order basis or by credit card and clear instructions are given with each issue of the guide on how to pay from anywhere in the world.

ENTERTAINMENT AND HOME COMFORTS

So, you've left the wonderful British weather behind, you've arrived in your new country and now it's time to settle into your new home.

Although discovering new interests and exploring new cultures will be fascinating and exciting, it can be quite hard initially and you may find that (for a short time at least) some familiar everyday links with home will really help you to adjust to your new surroundings.

This is where the internet is invaluable, especially if you are a partner based at home throughout the day and therefore without access to input and advice from work colleagues. Even if you've never used a computer before and can learn just enough to send e-mails and surf the web, then you will be able to find most of the information you need.

As well as keeping in touch easily with friends through e-mail, you can also go to the websites of most national and some local

British newspapers to really keep up to date with what's happening in your area back home and, if you're a keen sports person, to follow your local football or cricket team. You can also tune into BBC radio and your local radio stations. Sometimes, when feeling a little homesick, hearing a report on your local radio station about the traffic jams on the motorways you used to travel on or the icy road conditions can be all that's needed for a cure!

There are many excellent British expat clubs around the world and, even if there are none in your local area, you can still register and join the online forums. Here you can 'chat' to fellow expats, ask for advice and generally learn about other people's experiences. This can be really helpful if you have moved to a non-English-speaking country and the culture is very different to your own or even if it is English-speaking but 'not as we know it', as in the case of the United States or Australia, for example. It can be quite surprising to learn of so many differences in the same language, and quite a few humorous books have now been written on the subject, relating some of the embarrassing moments experienced by many Brits abroad!

Once you have settled in and got used to your new surroundings, your thoughts may turn to things you miss from home, such as certain foods or particular shops. There is a huge array of products now available to order on the internet and, as long as you order from a reputable company with a secure website, this should prove to be an easy, trouble-free transaction.

Regarding food, it can be quite daunting the first time you visit the supermarket in your new country, as you view rows and rows of goods, none of which is familiar to you. Although over time most people get used to the local produce, many expats take advantage of the online shopping services offered specifically for British expats, such as Expat Essentials, which will send out British food to nearly every country in the world. It may be something to use occasionally, when you feel like a treat from home or perhaps for more essential items like baby formula, as you will probably discover that your usual brand from the UK is not available overseas. For any family with young children, this is definitely worth checking and preparing for before you leave home, as the last thing you need is an upset baby. If you plan to take a large quantity of baby formula with you, it's also worth noting that some countries restrict the amount allowed, so it would be worthwhile to check with customs first, to make sure you can import the baby products you take with you or send on ahead.

Websites like Expat Essentials (www.expatessentials.com) also have a links page for other websites of interest to British expats, so this is an easy way of finding out all sorts of other information, without the need to spend days searching on Google. There is everything from British clubs to Visa consultants to buying property overseas. British embassies usually have a great selection of links on their websites too, so this is another area worth exploring.

A lot of the favourite high-street stores from Britain will only deliver within the UK, but you may be able to find a mail-forwarding company where you can have the goods delivered, and it will then charge you a small handling fee plus delivery to send them on to you. This can be especially useful for those everyday items like baby clothes, socks and underwear, where you know the quality is reliable and the fit is usually accurate. One thing to be aware of, though, is that most stores (depending on the type of goods) will not offer their usual guarantee or returns policy if the goods are being sent out of the UK. Sometimes, if it's not a particularly expensive item, it's still worth taking the risk, to be able to get the goods you're familiar with and you know that you like.

CDs are fairly universal, so you can continue to listen to your favourite music wherever you are. However, some DVDs and computer games have a different format and don't work overseas, so this is something worth checking before ordering. You may also find that a games console, such as PlayStation, Xbox, etc, taken from the UK will not play the games bought locally, so it's worth thoroughly checking the situation with any electrical or electronic items before you leave the UK or before you order from abroad. The manufacturers of these games consoles, such as Sony, can usually give you the right advice.

Lastly, wherever possible, try to learn as much as you can about the local people and their customs and their day-to-day accepted way of doing things, which may be quite different to the ways in the UK. It's always appreciated when someone tries to fit in and respects local tradition. People generally love to help too, so always ask for advice when appropriate. Probably the most important thing to remember is that, no matter how proud you are to be British (and rightly so), don't complain to your new friends about things being different to what you have at home and all the things you miss. This is where the online forums for expats are so good; you can let off steam to your fellow Brits about the things you don't like and get some good advice, without the risk of offending someone locally.

By following these simple guidelines, you should find that you'll settle into your new country in no time at all and then you can relax and enjoy all the wonderful new experiences you'll encounter. After a while, you'll probably wonder why on earth you missed Marmite or PG Tips so much, as you discover lots of fantastic new tastes to enjoy.

While your new home is likely to be a source of varied and new experiences, you might like to maintain some of the interests that you developed at home. The internet can provide an invaluable link for this. Football fans can follow their team's progress through the season by logging on to both official and unofficial websites. Chat forums can also keep you in contact with fellow fans. The internet might also be a way to find out if there are other expatriates or host-country fan clubs in your region, which could be a good way to meet people and set up a social network.

Using the internet to keep informed with both world and local news is also a new innovation. Many radio and TV companies now use it to broadcast. For example, CNN, Reuters and the BBC all have news information. Furthermore, you can listen to some radio programmes through the internet. The BBC has recently launched an audio online version of its news and entertainment programmes which can be found on the BBC site. National newspapers also use the internet and some, such as *The Daily Telegraph*, publish the whole day's paper on their website. Furthermore, local newspapers are also setting up websites, so it is quite possible to keep in touch with your local news – including football reports, and local issues such as education and government. A listing of websites can be found at the back of this book.

Sending for goods through mail order catalogues can make up for deficiencies in local shops when working abroad. Although many companies that provide goods by mail order confine their activities to the UK and will not send goods abroad (no doubt because of potential payment problems), there is nothing to stop you making arrangements to get catalogues through UK friends or relatives and ordering through them. Expatriates with young children are reported to find the Mothercare catalogue very useful. Harrods and Fortnum & Mason will send goods anywhere in the world and you can pay by credit card. Harrods also operate worldwide accounts, and franchise outlets in airports in some surprising places. However, e-commerce also means that receiving home comforts is no longer the complicated process it used to be and many large retail companies now have ordering facilities set up on their websites.

Checklist: Settling in

1. Try to organise domestic help as soon as possible and bring a few necessities with you.
2. Brief your domestic help as clearly as possible and identify duties from the start.
3. Make proper security arrangements and check that you have all your legal requirements for work, banking, medical help, etc.
4. Find out emergency numbers, including those of your consulate or embassy, and if you are relocating to a developing country, register with them as soon as possible.
5. Identify sources from where books and home comforts can be obtained, whether locally or internationally.
6. Seek out social networks through expatriate organisations, your employer or through the internet.
7. If you have not used the internet before, now is the time to become acquainted – it will be an invaluable source of information and support!

13 | Coming Home

Having completed a foreign assignment you might feel that your return home will be an uncomplicated affair. However, increasingly both companies and individuals are paying attention to the practical and psychological issues involved in repatriation. Not only do domestic issues, such as finding accommodation or dealing with tenants, need to be tackled, but career considerations and family issues need to be addressed. Furthermore, although you might feel confident about fitting back into professional and social networks, surprisingly some expatriates do experience a reverse culture shock on their return.

PERSONAL POSSESSIONS

If you are to reap the full benefit of a spell as a non-UK resident, planning for your return requires forethought and preparation, particularly in the matter of bringing back personal possessions. Price differentials between countries are no longer as great as they used to be, but there are still quite a number of places where, even taking freight into account, it is worth buying things like electronic or audiovisual equipment, even cars, locally and shipping them back home. In countries that operate exchange controls this may also be a possible way of taking out assets in the form of goods. But beware of the catch: unless you can show that an article has been used and owned for six months, you are liable for import duty – and VAT on top of that. It is no use asking an obliging vendor to provide backdated invoices, because if you are unlucky enough to come under investigation, customs officials check serial numbers as well as documents. Another thing to be aware of is that once your personal possessions, including cars, are imported without payment of import duty and VAT, they cannot be sold or disposed of within 12 months, or they become liable for both these taxes.

Even with well-used goods, you can be in for unforeseen costs unless you get your timing right. The problem is that possessions shipped back to the UK will not be released until their owner arrives home. You can get a relative to clear them on your behalf, but that person would be liable for provisional duty on their value which is only repaid when you yourself get back. It takes about a fortnight to clear goods through customs anyway, so you will need expert advice at the other end if you are to steer the difficult course between paying warehouse charges in the UK because the goods have arrived too soon, and finding yourself without the basic necessities of life because you have sent them off too late.

The most important thing, though, is that they should actually arrive. The cheapest form of shipping may not be the best. The right course of action is to find a local firm that has a reputable agent in the UK, and to make sure you get door-to-door insurance cover.

ACCOMMODATION

Providing you have gone through the correct tenancy arrangements, reclaiming your property should not be too complicated. However, be aware that if you return earlier than planned, and your tenants have time left on their agreement, you might have to find alternative accommodation for the outstanding tenancy period. In particular, under an Assured Shorthold Tenancy – unless your tenant agrees to move earlier – you will have to wait until the contract runs its course with two months' notice given after that period.

You should try to give the letting agents who are looking after your UK property at least three months' notice of your return, so that they can give due notice to the tenants. However, should you be unfortunate enough to come across a tenant who is unwilling to move on, it is possible to insure against legal and hotel costs.

FINDING A NEW JOB

Unless you have been sent out by a UK employer, the biggest problem in returning home can be in finding another job. Well before that point you should be sending your CV round to head-hunters who are always on the lookout for those with specialist qualifications. If you feel that you might have difficulty placing yourself on the job market on grounds of age or lack of specific skills, it may be worth consulting a career counsellor. They cannot 'find' you a job – and you should be wary of those who imply otherwise – but their advice, though not cheap, has been found to be a good investment by many mid-career jobseekers.

Returning employees are also faced with career dilemmas. An Arthur Andersen Survey as long ago as 1999 reported that 21 per cent of companies expect their returning employee to initiate the search for their next position. The proportion of companies offering help is unlikely to have risen. Of those companies that do offer help, under 10 per cent begin to look for a position for the expatriate a year before return and approximately 40 per cent used to do so 6–12 months before the end of the assignment, but the latter percentage has probably fallen. Indeed, this is precisely what stops many employees taking on a foreign assignment in the first place: a lack of career opportunities on their return. Employees who are unable to return to their former job have a number of options available to them, which are shown in Table 13.1. The outlook today for returning expatriates is probably worse than in 1999.

Chapter 3 deals with this subject in some depth. However, it is worth repeating at this point that the issue of reintegration should be raised before taking on an assignment. An employer who values the skills that have been developed abroad will also be thinking about how best to utilise them on your return. Leaving this to chance, though, is not a good idea. At least a year before your return you should be entering into a dialogue with your employer about career opportunities for your return. If your company provides a mentor, he or she should also be able to help create a constructive dialogue and repatriation process.

Table 13.1 Post-assignment options

Redundancy	50%
Re-assignment to another expatriate position	31%
Extension of current assignment	32%
Appointed 'special projects' in the home country	57%
Other	8%

Source: Arthur Andersen Expatriate Survey 1999

If you are able to settle back into your former job or one of equivalent status, it is also worth bearing in mind that time will have passed since you were last part of your home office team. Different faces, work practices and projects should be expected and it might take some time to readjust to your altered office environment. Do not expect that you will necessarily be welcome, as you will probably be affecting other people's career prospects.

The same 1999 Arthur Andersen Survey found that a mere 11 per cent of respondents offered some form of post-repatriation support during the 12 months after return, and this tended to be with tax compliance rather than personal support. None of the respondents gave any form of help with readjustment to home-country living and working, which, as the report's author Barry Page commented, 'is interesting, since inability to re-adapt to home-country office culture is ranked as the most common reason given by returning expatriates for leaving their company following their repatriation'.

Of course, returning expatriates have the option of moving into self-employment and this may be particularly attractive to those who have the opportunity to take early retirement on favourable terms. Since 2005, as final salary pension schemes are increasingly curtailed and changed to the 'money purchase' variety for the remainder of an employee's period of service, or where the employer requires increased contributions from pension scheme members to maintain benefits, it may make good sense to work for yourself and take your pension rights with you. As a returning expatriate, you may well have acquired skills and experience of foreign markets and industries that make you valuable as a consultant to companies that don't want to relocate their own staff – with the inevitable learning curve you went through when you took up your own assignment.

If you find that self-employment beckons, you should start researching the business opportunities and planning well before your return. In this day and age, there is no such thing as job security for life, and anyone over the age of 30 should have a 'Plan B' in the briefcase for self-employment or starting his or her own business. You might make a start by reading my book *Working for Yourself*, published by Kogan Page, and available at www.koganpage.com.

REVERSE CULTURE SHOCK

One of the most surprising aspects of returning home is the experience of reverse culture shock. Again, the passing of time needs to be taken into account. While you have been away things will have moved on in your home country and not only friends and family will have changed but your international experience will almost certainly have changed you as well. Your expectations might well have undergone a radical change abroad and coming home might mean that you, once again, have to re-adapt these to suit your circumstances. Much like any other major move, returning home requires a readjustment to new circumstances and time should be taken to absorb this process.

Fitting back into an office environment is one thing but it is also worth bearing in mind that partners and children might also experience difficulties settling back.

PREPARING THE FAMILY FOR RETURN

As with the move abroad, a trailing partner might well have to begin to search for another job on his or her return home. Beginning that search well in advance is well worth the time. Furthermore, enlightened companies are beginning to realise the need to provide information and support to enable partners to resettle. For example, Shell has 40 information centres worldwide providing information and support for partners. Children might also feel disorientated by returning home. Having to fit back into school and peer groups can be traumatic. Their experience of a different culture and returning to an unfamiliar environment might be disturbing for a period of time. Furthermore, they might not be able to return to their old school if places are scarce. Again, it is worth informing schools as early as possible about your return and to look for alternative arrangements should there be a lack of places. Children should be encouraged to keep in touch with home during a foreign assignment so that they are not completely out of step with changes on their return.

A foreign assignment is a fulfilling and life-enhancing experience. The re-adaption to home is part of that experience and its success or failure can affect the foreign experience in either a positive or negative way. Planning for your return is therefore a worthwhile process. Try to forewarn employers, tenants, schools and social contacts of your return well in advance. Keep your family in contact with friends and try to establish with your employer what job opportunities there are likely to be on your return. Most important of all, try to be patient with the new situation. It might be home, but home can also be a 'foreign' place if you have spent some years away.

Checklist: Coming home

1. Think about what goods might be worth buying to bring home and purchase six months before returning.
2. Plan the shipment of possessions carefully to coincide with your return or look into warehousing arrangements.
3. Inform your letting agents as soon as possible of the date you are to return in order to give your tenants as much notice as possible.
4. Look into short-term rental arrangements if you are unable to move back into your property straight away.
5. Discuss with your employer well in advance what plans there are for you on your return – this should ideally take place 12 months before return. If you are returning without a job, contact head-hunters and agencies as early as possible.
6. Develop a 'Plan B' for self-employment in case you find that there is no acceptable job opportunity on your return.
7. Be prepared for reverse culture shock and give yourself time to become accustomed to changes in your home and work environment.
8. Contact schools in advance and make contact with your children's friends before returning home.
9. Contact partners' support centres run by your employer to identify career opportunities.

Part Five:

Website Directory of Useful Contacts

The websites listed are those identified at the time of going to print. Due to the dynamic nature of the internet, variations in content and changes of address might occur. The publishers cannot take responsibility for the content of the websites listed but have tried to ensure, where possible, that the material is of a suitable nature. However, an exemplary illustration of what can be found on the internet is the *Electronic Telegraph*'s expatriate website, Global Network, which offers advice, links and country profiles. It can be found at www.telegraph.co.uk or www.global network.co.uk.

INTERNET DIRECTORIES AND SEARCH ENGINES

Alta Vista
http://uk.altavista.com
Britannica Internet Guide
www.ebig.com
Excite Search
www.excite.com
www.excite.co.uk
Google
www.google.com
Google Groups
http://groups.google.com
Search tool for finding news groups.
HotBot
www.hotbot.com
The Lists/Topica
www.lists.com
Search tool for e-mail discussion groups and e-mail publishing.
Regional Directory
www.edirectory.com
Listing of regional web directories.
UK Directory
www.ukdirectory.co.uk
Who Where
www.whowhere.com
Directory of e-mail addresses to help you keep in contact with friends, family and organisations.
Yahoo!
www.yahoo.com
http://uk.yahoo.com

JOB OPPORTUNITIES
Internet resources

America's Job Bank
www.ajb.dni.us
Extensive database of current vacancies in the United States.

Cadremploi
www.cadremploi.fr
France's leading management career site.
Career Builder.com
www.careerbuilder.com
Provides regional breakdowns of salary information.
Career Resource Centre
www.careers.org
Index of US and Canadian careers-related websites, with more than 8,000 links to related sites.
CareersInsite
www.careersinsite.org
US university site with over 1,000 links to job searching sites.
Cool Works
www.coolworks.com
Provides links to details of 'cool' jobs with the emphasis on the United States. For example, jobs in national and state parks, ski resorts and ranches. Visa restrictions are problematic for Europeans, but it is worth having a look at this site.
JobHunters Bible
www.jobhuntersbible.com
Reviews of US guidance sites with links to them.
Job Site
www.jobsite.co.uk
Directory of major UK and European recruiters, mainly in IT and human resource management.
The Monster Board
www.monster.com
Invaluable resource on international job opportunities and country-specific information. Sites in Canada, Australia, Belgium, The Netherlands and the United States.
Prospects Web
www.prospects.ac.uk
Careers information for graduates with overseas sites offering vacancy information.
The Riley Guide to Employment Opportunities and Job Resources on the Internet
www.rileyguide.com
Worldwide vacancies with emphasis on the United States.
Sciencejobs.com
www.sciencejobs.com
International scientific employment opportunities.
SYO-Guiden
www.syoguiden.com
Swedish site with links to career guidance sites worldwide.
TV Jobs
www.tvjobs.com
US TV companies offering intern or work experience or placements.

Media

BioMed*Scientist*
www.biomedscientistjobs.com
International life science and medical recruitment site. Vacancies from *The Scientist* and *BioMed* journals.

British Medical Journal
www.bmjcareers.com
Medical vacancies.

Careers in Construction
www.careersinconstruction.com
Vacancies from *The Architects' Journal*, *Construction News* and *New Civil Engineer*, updated weekly. Links to other sites of specialist journals.

The Daily Telegraph
www.telegraph.co.uk
Online version of full paper with recruitment vacancies worldwide.

E&P Directory of Online Newspapers
www.editorandpublisher.com
Reference resource including newspapers on the web and proprietary online services. Listed by country with search facilities for specific publications, locations or attributes. Also provides a career centre which boasts an extensive job search facility.

Emap
www.emap.com
Publishers of a wide range of trade and specialist magazines with recruitment sections.

Expat Network
www.expatnetwork.co.uk
Publishes *Nexus* and offers support service for expats and a register of those looking for work abroad which is sent to recruiters.

Financial Times
www.ft.com
Finance- and business-related vacancies.

The Guardian Unlimited
http://jobs.guardian.co.uk
Vacancies in wide range of occupational areas.

Inkpot Newspaper Links
http://inkpot.com/news/majint.html
Links to international newspapers by country and region.

Irish Times
www.irishtimesjobs.com
Searchable site for jobs in Ireland.

Nature
www.nature.com/naturejobs
International science job listings, updated weekly.

Overseas Job Express
www.overseasjobs.com
Newspaper carrying 1,500 job vacancies and information about working abroad every two weeks.

Physics World Jobs
http://careers.iop.org
Part of the UK's Institute of Physics site with job and research opportunities.

ResortJobs
www.resortjobs.com
Also produced by Overseas Job Express, a database of worldwide resort jobs. Includes ski and snowboarding resorts, national parks, cruise ships, hotels and restaurants.

Summer Jobs
www.summerjobs.com
Also produced by Overseas Job Express, a database of seasonal and summer jobs.

Recruitment consultancies and employment agencies

Au pair JobMatch
www.aupairs.co.uk
Search by country and nationality of families for worldwide au pair vacancies.

Crewseekers International
www.crewseekers.co.uk
Work found for amateur crews for leisure sailing, cruising and racing.

Engineering Production Planning Limited
www.epp.co.uk
Agency with offices in Europe, Singapore and the United States. Specialises in vacancies in aerospace, oil and gas, water, power generation, nuclear engineering, production, defence, communications, chemical processing, civil engineering and manufacturing.

Hays International
www.hays.com
International vacancies.

Malla Technical Recruitment Consultancy
www.malla.com
Specialising in engineering placements worldwide.

Michael Page International
www.michaelpage.com
Offices in the Americas, Australasia and Europe, specialising in accounting, banking and finance.

Pilot Select
www.pilotselect.com
Matches pilots with airlines looking for crews.

Reed
www.reed.co.uk
Vacancies, careers information and links to career resources worldwide.

Reed Finance
www.reed.co.uk/finance

Robert Walters
www.robertwalters.com
International accounting and finance recruitment agency.

Veterinary Locums Worldwide
www.vetlocums.com
Site for vets looking for short-term work in practices, wildlife projects or with exotic animals.

Professional Associations

British Medical Association
www.bma.org.uk

Information and advice on working abroad for BMA members.
Institute of Physics
www.iop.org
Physics-related vacancies.
Royal College of Nursing
www.rcn.org.uk
Information and advice on working abroad for RCN members.

Organisations

The British Council
www.britishcouncil.org
Teaching opportunities and voluntary work overseas. Recruits EFL teachers for its own Language Centres.
Committee on the Status of Women in Physics
www.aps.org/educ/cswp
Arm of the American Physical Society. Information on dual-science-career jobs.
Council on International Educational Exchange
www.ciee.org
Work experience, short-term jobs and worldwide exchange programmes for students and recent graduates.
Doctors without Borders
www.doctorswithoutborders.org
Opportunities for medically trained personnel to work in developing countries.
European Commission
www.cec.org.uk/work/index/htm
Commission's current vacancies for English-speaking candidates.
The International Health Exchange
www.ihe.org.uk
Health personnel for programmes in developing countries.
Search Beat
www.searchbeat.com/energyjobs.htm
Worldwide jobs in the petroleum industry.
United Nations
http://unjobs.org
Vacancy board for UN departments worldwide.

Teaching English as a Foreign Language

The British Council
See Organisations.
The Centre for British Teachers
www.cfbt.com
Teaching vacancies in Brunei, Oman and Turkey and educational specialists in Eastern Europe, Africa, Asia and India.
Council on International Educational Exchange
See Organisations.
ELT Job Vacancies
www.jobs.edufind.com

Teaching English as a Foreign Language posts worldwide.
International House
www.ihlondon.com
Recruits teachers for 100 schools in 26 countries.
i-to-i
www.i-to-i.com
i-to-i provides language courses, such as TEFL, for travellers along with volunteer placements around the world.
TEFL
www.tefl.co.uk
Teaching English as a Foreign Language courses.
TEFL.com
www.tefl.com
Teaching English as a Foreign Language job database with links to worldwide employment vacancies.

Voluntary work

British Council
See Organisations.
i-to-i
See TEFL.
Voluntary Service Overseas
www.vso.org.uk
Opportunities in 58 countries in education, health, technical trades, engineering and other fields.

International companies

BDO Stoy Hayward
www.bdo.co.uk/taxservices
A cohesive worldwide network of specialists providing immigration, tax and social security advice to expatriates and their employers.
Boeing
www.boeing.com
Aviation giant offers internships for college students at US institutions.
British Airways
www.britishairwaysjobs.com
Cabin crew, IT and sales vacancies.
GlaxoSmithKline
www.gsk.com/careers/joinus.htm
Access to both UK and US searches for current vacancies in this pharmaceutical company.
Hewlett-Packard
www.jobs.hp.com
IT giant with online application forms.
IBM
www.ibm.com
US site has links to global recruitment.

Integra Global
www.integraglobal.com
International medical insurance providers.
Lloyds TSB
www.lloydstsb.com
International banking.
Microsoft
www.microsoft.com/careers
Information vacancies at the company's different locations.
Shell International
www.shell.com
Superb website with access to expatriate information on its 'OUTPOST' (www.outpost expat.nl) and Spouses Support Network websites (see Expat networks).
Standard Bank
www.standardbank.com
International banking.

COUNTRY-SPECIFIC DATA
Political information

Foreign and Commonwealth Office
www.fco.gov.uk
Travel Advice Unit provides up-to-the-minute information on political upheaval, natural disasters and epidemics worldwide.
United Nations
www.un.org
Information on countries in the UN.
US Department of State Travel Advisories
http://travel.state.gov/travel
Up-to-the-minute information in the same vein as the Foreign and Commonwealth Office.

Economic data

CIA FactBook
www.cia.gov/cia/publications/factbook
Country breakdown with economic, political, geographic and demographic information available.
Economics Departments, Institutes and Research Centers in the World (EDIRC – University of Connecticut)
http://edirc.repec.org
Index of economic institutions on the web.
Financial Times Country Briefs
http://surveys.ft.com
Superb country surveys providing developments and detailed information on regions and countries, including economic indicators and company activity and performance details.

Union Bank of Switzerland
www.ubs.com
Produces comparative survey 'Prices and Earnings Around the Globe' detailing costs
and earnings in 53 countries.

Business guides

Department of Trade and Industry Export Publications
www.dti.gov.uk/export.control/publications.htm
Publications aimed at businesses abroad and for intending expatriates.
Hong Kong and Shanghai Banking Corporation
www.hsbc.com/businessprofiles
Publishes 'Business Profiles' aimed at companies and private individuals and
contains useful information on living conditions.

General information

The Centre for International Briefing
www.farnhamcastle.com
Cultural and business briefings covering all regions of the world. Also customised
programmes and language tuition.
ECA International
www.eca-international.com
Relocation company with excellent resources and country briefings worldwide.
Expat Network
www.expatnetwork.co.uk
Among other services provides location reports to members.
Expedia
www.expedia.co.uk
Many links to other travel sites.

Continent-specific information

Africa

Africaonline
www.africaonline.com
Information on African countries.
AllAfrica.com
http://allafrica.com
African news and information on countries.
Commonwealth Institute
www.commonwealth.org.uk
Information on member states of the Commonwealth.
www.kenyaweb.com
General information on the culture, history and life in Kenya.
Yahoo!
http://travel.yahoo.com/p-travelguide-191500003-africa_vacations-i
Search engine directory of information on the region.

America

US Census Bureau
www.census.gov
US statistics with links.
Yahoo!
http://travel.yahoo.com/p-travelguide-191501863-united_states_vacations-i
Search engine directory of information on the region.

Asia

Commonwealth Institute
See above.
East Asia Business Services
www.shef.ac.uk/eltc/services/eabs
Tailor-made briefings for expatriates going to Japan, China, Korea or other East Asian countries.
School of Oriental and African Studies
www.soas.ac.uk
Briefing and language service, open briefings on Japan and China, two-day Japan Business Orientation programme.
Yahoo!
http://travel.yahoo.com/p-travelguide-191500005-asia_vacations-i
Search engine directory of information on the region.

Europe

European Commission
www.europa.eu.int
www.cec.org.uk
Factsheets and information on working and living in the European Union.
Yahoo!
http://travel.yahoo.com/p-travelguide-191500008-europe_vacations-i
Search engine directory of information on the region.

Middle East

ArabNet
www.arab.net
Yahoo!
http://travel.yahoo.com/p-travelguide-191500009-middle_east_vacations-i
Search engine directory of information on the region.

Language tuition

Berlitz (UK) Ltd
www.berlitz.co.uk
Language tuition.

EXPAT NETWORKS

British in America
www.britishinamerica.com
Expats in the US link-up.

Britnet
www.british-expats.com
International site for British living abroad.

Brits Abroad
www.britsabroad.co.uk

Diplomatic Service Families Association
www.fco.gov.uk
Promotes the interest and welfare of spouses of serving and retired diplomatic service officers. Provides a link between those at home and abroad.

Escapeartist
www.escapeartist.com
Superb website with links to expat forums, country-specific data, advice on relocation and much more.

Expat Exchange
www.expatexchange.com
Comprehensive information source on moving overseas, tax and finance plus much more. Runs an expat network.

Expat Forum
www.expatforum.com
Chat forums in 24 country-specific areas, along with other areas of interest to expats.

Expatica
www.expatica.com
Well-resourced website for expatriates living in Belgium, France, Spain, Germany and The Netherlands.

Expat Network
www.expatnetwork.co.uk
Publishes *Nexus* and offers a support service for expats.

Expat Online
www.expat-online.com
Network for expats living in Belgium.

Expats in Brussels
www.expatsinbrussels.com
Interactive site for the expatriate community in Brussels.

Federation of American Women's Clubs Overseas, Inc
www.fawco.org

OUTPOST
www.outpostexpat.nl
Shell International's superb expat website.

Spouse Employment Centre
www.incnetwork.demon.co.uk
Shell International's website providing information to partners who wish to work or develop their skills during expatriation.

TCK
www.tckworld.com

Website for parents of 'Third Culture Kids' (TCK – expat children) which aims to enable parents to understand the culture shock their children may experience whilst living abroad.

EDUCATION

British Dyslexia Association
www.bda-dyslexia.org.uk
Advice on the teaching of dyslexic children.

Cambridge Education Associates
www.cea.co.uk
Provides free educational advice as well as a comprehensive guardianship service.

Clarendon International Education
www.clarendon.uk.com
Offers guardianship services.

Department for Education and Skills
www.dfes.gov.uk
Information on maintained boarding schools.

European Council of International Schools
www.ecis.org
Details of 400 international schools and website access to International Schools Directory.

Gabbitas Educational Consultants
www.gabbitas.co.uk
Advice on a selection of suitable schools. Also offers guardianship services.

Gabbitas.net
www.gabbitas.net
Excellent site that contains a fully searchable directory of English-speaking international and special schools.

International Baccalaureate Organisation
www.ibo.org

OCR – Oxford Cambridge and RSA Examination Board
www.ocr.org.uk
Administers the AICE curriculum.

National Extension College
www.nec.ac.uk
Offers GCSE and A-level correspondence courses.

The New School, Rome
www.newschoolrome.com

Universities and Colleges Admissions Service
www.ucas.com
Central agency for all UK universities.

World-wide Education Service
www.wesworldwide.com
Information on overseas schools.

The World-wide Education Service (Home School) Ltd
www.weshome.demon.co.uk
Specialises in teaching children with special needs.

HEALTH ADVICE

AXA PPP healthcare
www.axappphealthcare.co.uk
BUPA International
www.bupa.co.uk
Medical insurance worldwide.
Hospital for Tropical Diseases
www.thehtd.org
For access to Health Information for Overseas Travel.
International SOS Assistance
www.internationalsos.com
Provides emergency help in a time of crisis.
Medical Advisory Service for Travellers Abroad (MASTA)
www.masta.org
Offers health briefs on 250 countries.
Reuters Health
www.reutershealth.com/en/

ENTERTAINMENT

Books

Amazon Books
www.amazon.com and www.amazon.co.uk
Delivery of over 2 million titles worldwide.
Internet Public Library
www.ipl.org
Online access to various publications.

Newspapers

The Daily Telegraph
www.telegraph.co.uk
Almost entire content of daily newspaper.
The Guardian
www.guardian.co.uk
Selected cuttings.
The Sunday Times
www.sunday-times.co.uk
Full content.
The Times
www.timesonline.co.uk
Full content.

Sport

Skysports
www.skysports.com
News on a range of sports.

Sportsweb
www.sportsweb.com
As above.
Yahoo!
http://sports.yahoo.com
Comprehensive listings of websites covering every type of sport imaginable.

Television and radio

BBC News
www.news.bbc.co.uk
BBC Online
www.bbc.co.uk
Radio and World Service programmes online with audio versions.
CNN
www.cnn.com
Soap Digest
www.soapoperadigest.com
Keep up to date with your favourite soaps.

Music, DVDs and Videos

Amazon Music, DVDs and Videos
www.amazon.com and amazon.co.uk
Delivery of over 2 million new and used CDs, cassettes, DVDs and videos worldwide.
CD Wow
www.cd-wow.com
International music, DVD and games site that delivers worldwide.
MTV
www.mtv.com
Online music site.

USEFUL MISCELLANEOUS WEBSITES

Allied Pickfords
www.alliedpickfords.co.uk
International removals.
Cybercafe Search Engine
www.cybercaptive.com
Cybercafe locations worldwide to ensure internet access.
Department for Environment, Food and Rural Affairs
www.defra.gov.uk
Advice on the transportation of animals overseas.
Expatnetwork
www.expatnetwork.co.uk
Gift service to send gifts or flowers to friends and family.
Expedia
www.expedia.co.uk
Travel links.

Fedex
www.fedex.com
Website of Federal Express for your freight needs.

Foreign Languages for Travellers
www.travlang.com/languages
Phrases in many languages.

Going-There.com
www.going-there.com
International relocation company with offices based in the UK and abroad.

Kropla
www.kropla.com
Extremely useful site with worldwide electrical and telephone information. Details of electric plugs and voltages used.

Mastercard/Cirrus ATM Locator
www.mastercard.com/cardholderservices/atm
Find automated teller machine in your new location.

MonsterMoving
www.moving.com
Comprehensive array of moving-related services and resources.

VISA ATM Locator
visa.via.infonow.net/locator/global
Find automated teller machine in your new location.

Visa Service
www.visaservice.co.uk
Specialises in processing applications for business visas and passports.

Worldwide Holiday and Festival Page
http://www.holidayfestival.com
Public holidays throughout the world.

Worldwide weather forecasts
www.intellicast.com
Local weather around the globe.

XE.com
www.xe.com
Currency converter.

Index

Index of Advertisers

Contact Details for Advertisers

AXA PPP Healthcare
Head Office
Phillips House
Crescent Road
Tunbridge Wells
Kent TN1 2PL
Tel: +44 (0) 1892 550817
Website: www.axappphealthcare.co.uk/wa

British Council
10 Spring Gardens
London SW1A 2BN
Tel: 0207 3894931
E-mail: teacher.vacancies@britishcouncil.org
Website: http://trs.britishcouncil.org

Bupa International
Russell House
Russell Mews
Brighton
East Sussex BN12NR
Tel: +44 (0) 1273 208181
Website: www.bupa-intl.com

Crown Relocations
19 Stonefield Way
Ruislip
Middlesex HA4 0BJ
Tel: 0800 919940
E-mail: enquiries.uk@crownrelo.com
Website: www.moveoverseas.co.uk

Dolphin Movers Ltd
2 Haslemere Business Centre
Lincoln Way
Enfield
Middlesex EN1 1TE
Tel: 0800 032 9777
E-mail: sales@dolphinmovers.com
Wesbite: www.dolphinmovers.com

Expacare
Columbia Centre
Market Street
Bracknell
Berkshire RG12 1JG
Tel: +44 (0) 1344 381650
Website: www.expacare.com

Livingabroad Magazine
The Media Company Publications Ltd
21 Royal Circus
Edinburgh
Scotland EH3 6TL
Tel: 0131 226 7766
Website: www.livingabroadmagazine.com

Lloyds TSB Offshore Banking
PO Box 160
25 New Street
St. Helier
Jersey JE4 8RG
Tel: 01624 638000
E-mail: newaccs@lloydstsb-offshore.com
Website: www.lloydstsb-offshore.com/workingabroad

No1currency
11 Glenfinlas Street
Charlotte Square,
Edinburgh
EH3 6AQ
Tel: 08000 237 037
Wesbite: www.no1currency.com

Oxford University Press
Great Clarendon Street
Oxford OX2 6DP
Tel: +44 (0) 1536 741017
E-mail: bookorders.uk@oup.com
Website: www.askoxford.com/languages/takeoffin

Routledge
2 Park Square
Milton Park
Abingdon
Oxford OX14 4RN
Tel: +44 (0) 20 7017 6284
E-mail: colloquials@routledge.com
Website: www.routledge.com/colloquials

Strathallan School
Forgandenny
Perth PH2 9EG
Tel: 01738 812546
E-mail: admissions@strathallan.co.uk
Website: www.strathallan.co.uk

World Wide Education Service
WES Home School
Waverley House
Penton
Carlisle
Cumbria CA6 5QU
Tel: +44 (0) 1228 577123
E-mail: office@weshome.demon.co.uk
Website: www.weshome.demon.co.uk

ALSO AVAILABLE FROM KOGAN PAGE

"For any business thinking of doing business in China, the information in this book will make it a 'must read'. The practical advice it contains, written and edited by experts, will be of enormous assistance – and I commend it to you."

Miles Templeman, Director General, Institute of Directors

ISBN: 978 0 7494 5062 5   Hardback   2008

Order online now at www.koganpage.com

Sign up for regular e-mail updates on new
Kogan Page books in your interest area

ALSO AVAILABLE FROM KOGAN PAGE

"An impressive collection of articles and essays giving best practice advice on all aspects of managing risk."
Manager

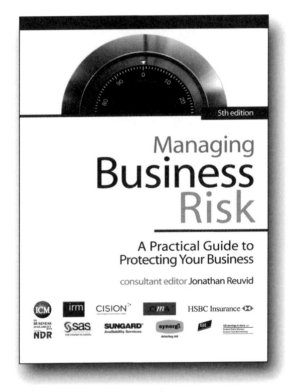

ISBN: 978 0 7494 5059 5   Hardback   2008